It's No Secret

It's No Secret

FROM NAS TO JAY-Z, FROM SEDUCTION TO SCANDAL,
A HIP-HOP HELEN OF TROY TELLS ALL

· · · · · · · · · ·

CARMEN BRYAN

VH1 BOOKS   POCKET BOOKS

NEW YORK   LONDON   TORONTO   SYDNEY

POCKET BOOKS, a division of Simon & Schuster, Inc.
1230 Avenue of the Americas, New York, NY 10020

First VH-1 Books/Pocket Books trade paperback edition November 2007

POCKET and colophon are registered trademarks of
Simon & Schuster, Inc.

For information regarding special discounts for bulk purchases, please contact
Simon & Schuster Special Sales at 1-800-456-6798 or business@simonandschuster.com.

Designed by Mary Austin Speaker

Manufactured in the United States of America

10 9 8 7 6 5 4 3 2 1

ISBN-13: 978-1-4165-3266-8
ISBN-10:   1-4165-3266-8
ISBN-13: 978-1-4165-3720-5 (pbk)
ISBN-10:   1-4165-3720-1 (pbk)

This work is a memoir. It reflects the author's present recollections of her experiences over a period of years. Certain names and identifying characteristics have been changed. Dialogue and other events have been re-created and conflated to convey the substance of what was said or what occurred, but are not intended to be a perfect representation.

This book is dedicated to single mothers and their struggle.
You're not alone.

ACKNOWLEDGMENTS

. . . .

FIRST AND FOREMOST I'D like to thank God the Creator, whose love never ceases to amaze me. My darling daughter, Destiny, whom I live for! My parents, Sha Sha and Papa Lenny, I wouldn't trade either of you for the world! My brother, Van—told you I was gonna be famous! My sisters, Janine and Fifi; my entire family; all of my friends (there are just too many to name and I don't want to leave anyone out); and all my pre-orders, it was you guys who got the ball rolling. Thank you so much!

My Team: Seven, here we go again! Tanell, thanks for all your help. Rennette and Shell Dimez—True Riders! Jeff, Dula, Stacy and Triche Christmon of Star Link Media; Denise, Doggest & Dell; Dexter of Clever Concepts; Court Digga, Will, Nana. My Glam Squad: Tonya, Jewrel, JoJo and Michelle.

Special thanks to Simon & Schuster and staff, VH1 and Pocket Books and staff, Lauren McKenna, Megan McKeever, Ian Klienart, Lindsay Jurgenson, Matt Greenberg, Elliot Wilson, Minya Oh, the G-Unit staff, Violator Management and staff.

I'd like to especially thank 50! Your words of wisdom, kindness and encouragement made this all possible.

And last but not least, Vanessa Satten, someone whose dedication, sincere thoughts and actions made one of my wildest dreams come true. You will always be a very dear friend to me. Shout out to the Satten family!

CONTENTS

· · · · · · · · · ·

CONTENTS

It's No Secret

Prologue

. . . .

"CARM, IS HE TALKING ABOUT YOU?"

Nas's insistent voice penetrated the fog in my head. I must have picked up the ringing telephone in my sleep. Had it awakened our daughter, Destiny, too?

"What?" My bedside clock read midnight. It was 3 A.M. for Nas in New York. Uh-oh. Whatever prompted this call was troubling enough to keep him awake.

"I keep hearing about this Memphis Bleek song with Jay-Z. It's supposed to be about you."

The song was news to me, but at the mention of Shawn's name my heart sank down to my stomach, which tightened into knots. I sat up in bed and tossed aside the silk comforter. With the movement the diamond on my left hand caught a silvery ray of moonlight. I took a deep breath and calmed down. Nas and I were finally getting married. This was no time to panic.

"What song?" I asked, as neutrally as possible.

" 'Is That Your Chick.' Carm, it's getting harder and harder for me to ignore the rumors about you and this dude—"

"They are just rumors, Nas." I put on what I hoped was a persuasively reasonable tone. "People talk. I put up with rumors about who you're supposed to be with all the time. Foxy, Beyoncé, Mary J. Every week they're saying it's someone new. You're just going to have to charge it to the game like I do."

Nas was silent. I could almost hear him balancing it out in his mind. On one side, there was my comforting explanation. A big part of him wanted to believe it. On the other hand, there was the growing weight of his suspicion. Nas wasn't exactly buying my little speech, but he let things drop for the moment. We hung up and I lunged for the bathroom, where I was sick.

• • •

Nas was very competitive in that he had two part-time jobs: he spent half his time talking up himself and the other half talking down others. In public, Nas tended to be more low-key and aloof than other entertainers. But at home, he was extremely opinionated and vocal about his peers' artistic efforts. Even if he was cool with someone personally, Nas always had a raw comment about their music. For example: in my opinion, Foxy Brown is the most talented female MC. Most will agree Foxy wears the crown, hands down. Not Nas. "You could just throw a few ingredients in a bowl, stir, and come up with another Foxy," he would rant. He had criticism of just about anyone. He would say Ja Rule was biting DMX's style, or Fat Joe was corny. These reviews always led up to the same point: "There is no real talent out there." The only lyricist Nas considered to be in his league was the late B.I.G. Nas's battle with Jay-Z was as much one of words as of the heart. I'd started seeing Jay finally doing to Nas what he'd been doing to me for years.

Nas and Jay-Z always had this bizarre competition. Nas would make comments to me like, "I don't remember that nigga being no ill drug dealer." In fact no one with any real credibility could confirm Jay-Z's "back in the day" drug dealer/baller status. Exaggeration is standard in the music industry. But according to Nas, Jay-Z had no merit to his claims and not one defender.

"Carm, this nigga Jay is so shallow," Nas would say. "He's a surface MC. He's plastic on stage. That's bad enough. But he doesn't even know what he's talking about. He hasn't done half the shit he's talking about in his rhymes. I don't believe him. Period."

Still, I couldn't imagine what might have motivated this "Is That Your Chick" song. Naturally Shawn would appear on Memphis Bleek's single—a fellow artist on the Roc-A-Fella label. And the song certainly could have something to do with me. Throughout our clandestine relationship Shawn had made many references to me in his lyrics. But he had never said anything negative or explicit and had never used his relationship with me to taunt Nas.

This was turning into an urban soap opera with me in a leading role as the femme fatale. I had to hear this Memphis Bleek song. After a few calls to friends in New York, I found someone to play the song for me over the phone. It went "How foul is she? And you wifed her" and talked about how he put the condom on "tighter."

At first I thought, *Psss . . . I don't know who Shawn's referring to, but he damn sure ain't talking about me!* The lyrics were rather racy and described a type of liaison that was the exact opposite of our relationship.

Shawn's disparaging lyrics gave no indication of the solid friendship we'd shared over the years. Not to mention the fact that it took a good year before we even became lovers or that I had recently been pregnant by him—'cause he didn't wear a condom at all, let alone tight enough.

After listening to the song, it was evident that the record was designed to take a direct stab at Nas, making me a casualty of this ongoing and highly publicized strife.

I tried to put things in perspective and take it like a hard-nosed realist, but I couldn't feign callousness. Shawn's actions were a complete disappointment. Instead of being hurt, I was enraged. I knew what I had to do before this thing went any further. I had to bring Nas up to speed. It was time to reveal the truth, once and for all.

Throughout the next day, Nas gathered evidence that the song referred to me. That night he called back for another round of questions. As I quietly deflected them, I walked by Destiny's room to make sure she was asleep, then headed downstairs. I walked down the stairs with the cordless phone to my ear, my forehead breaking out into a sweat. My heart was racing, my breathing became heavy and my stomach was in knots. I even said a quick little prayer and turned off all the lights as if darkness provided an escape.

After some anxious pacing between the bathroom and

kitchen, I ended up in front of my bathroom mirror, in darkness. My reflection was a vague silhouette, just barely visible. I was so tired of misrepresenting myself, of sneaking out, of lying and denying the truth. Of course, Nas had long done the same thing. It had been a rough and rocky nine years for us. But for all our drama, we were inextricably linked—we had a daughter and deep, deep history together. I couldn't let Shawn belittle Nas as a man. Nas deserved to have a fighting chance.

"Nas, it's true." My words tumbled out. "The rumors are true. I have been seeing Jay-Z."

"Carm, how could you?" Nas asked in disbelief. "Why that nigga? I can't believe what you're telling me right now."

"Nas, I'm sorry." I choked out my apology as I started to cry. "I am so sorry." I had always thought that when this day finally came I would feel vindicated. For so long I had craved the taste of bittersweet revenge. Nas would finally feel what I had felt over the years. But this was completely different. I felt horrible, not for my actions, but because I had hurt Nas and he was suffering from tremendous heartache. It just wasn't what I'd envisioned.

Nas was unmoved by my sobbing regret. He wanted details. "How long have you been fucking with this dude?"

"It's been a minute," I answered. Even though I'd resolved to tell him everything, it took a while to get my courage up.

"How long is a minute, Carm?"

"Like five years."

"*Five years! Five years, Carm?* What the fuck is wrong with you? What were you thinking? You mean all this time I been hearing rumors about you and this nigga, brushing them off like, 'Nah, not Carm. She may do her thing but she would never disrespect me like that. . . . Where did you meet this nigga at?"

"We met at a club in the city. It started as a friendship. Was for a year before we slept together."

Nas sucked his teeth. "I don't give a fuck if it took you ten years to sleep with him. You're supposed to be my wife, that shit wasn't supposed to happen, Carm! I don't deserve this. I want to know everything! You ever been to his crib?"

"Yes."

"You ever been to a hotel with him?"

"No. We always hang out at his crib."

"Did you ever take my car to go see this nigga?" I thought to myself, *What kind of question is that?* But I continued to answer.

"Uh huh."

These intimate details would give Nas enough material to spin some elaborately jealous story lines in his mind. Still, I had to answer the questions to prevent his imagination from getting the best of him. He would drive himself crazy with speculation if he didn't have this chance to grill me.

"Does he hold you at night?"

"Yes."

He hesitated. I realized what he really wanted to ask. Guys may feign disinterest about the matter, but they're all anxious to know: Is he bigger than me? For the moment Nas avoided the size question.

"Did you go down on him?" he asked.

"Once."

"Once, I don't believe that! You're such a fucking slut! I can't believe you sucked that nigga's dick, Carm. Come on, you're gonna tell me you only did it once. You're such a fucking liar."

"It's true. You can ask him."

"What? Ask him? Carm, I'm gonna kill that nigga! I fucking hate you!"

Nas hung up on me. I called back. He just kept screaming through his extensive vocabulary of derogative terms: I was a slut, a whore, a dirty bitch and more. He hung up, but then immediately called back, hoping to find some release in another diatribe. It had the opposite effect: Ranting only sustained his sense of violation, kept his feelings raw. We went back and forth with a few more rounds of confession and condemnation until he finally stopped answering the phone. Nas was done with me for the night. Maybe forever.

I turned on the bathroom light and looked in the mirror, still crying. Tears seemed to be washing away my features, making an anonymous mask of my face. So I had finally confessed to Nas. I looked at myself a little more closely. It was time for me to get real with myself.

I was crying tears of frustration. Shawn had stripped me of the opportunity to divulge our relationship in my own private way. I was mortified that Nas found out in such a public manner. But that's the way it goes down in a love triangle, the unholiest of trinities.

I stared in the mirror until I finally stopped crying, then washed away the residue of my tears. Facing the truth gave me a new clarity. Self-realization smoothed my forehead and con-viction strengthened my jaw. I was naïve enough to believe the uncovering of my affair with Jay-Z would bring closure to my re-lationship with Nas. I was ready for it to end.

But it wasn't the end. In fact, it was only the beginning.

CHAPTER 1

In the Beginning

. . . .

IT'S ALWAYS THE SAME with beginnings. When I first met Nas, everything seemed possible. Everything was possible. It was early December 1992. I was twenty years old, looking for refuge from a troubling situation in New Haven, Connecticut. A quick trip back to Flushing, New York, would alleviate the building tension. My brother Van and our childhood friend Paulie, a.k.a. Large Professor, had taken over the lease at 7C, the very apartment we'd grown up in since middle school when we first moved to Flushing. My mother, whom we called Sha Sha, had recently moved in with my grandparents, now that they were getting older and could use the help. Van and Paulie had transformed the space into a bachelor pad/sound lab. They'd painted the walls chocolate brown, except for the kitchen, which was blue and psychedelic orange. The kitchen table was reincarnated as a turntable stand. Pots, pans, plates and silverware had been discarded. There was nothing cooking in that kitchen now but beats, considering they were both aspiring producers. Over in the corner a shopping cart overflowed with empty beer and soda bottles. Studio equipment dominated the apartment, with crates of records and clothes crammed in between. It was a budding producer's dream pad.

I didn't exactly tell Van what was going on with my life in New Haven, or anyone for that matter, except that I needed to move back to New York. Without any questions or hesitation my brother offered me his bedroom. Typical Van! He was still the generous and caring person he had been growing up.

On my second day home, Paulie pulled me aside. "There's someone I want you to meet. He's from Queensbridge, I've known him for a while and he's cool."

"Not looking," I told Paulie. My romantic life in Connecticut was already complicated enough, thank you. I definitely didn't need another one of those.

Later that day, by the time I got home from my cousin Felicia's house, which was right across the street, I'd forgotten all about Paulie's suggested set-up. There were four or five new faces in the apartment, though I could barely make them out in the smoky haze. They'd probably had blunts burning for hours. It was customary; everyone usually pooled in on a $25-an-hour cab and headed uptown to buy as much weed as possible. Usually they spent more on the transportation than the weed; with five or six guys passing, half the trees were gone by the time they were home. Weed pilgrimages were therefore a daily necessity. I wasn't much of a smoker yet and just hoped there'd be no repeat of the previous night's episode. Our doorman had come to the apartment to ask us to keep the noise down. "You might want to wedge that towel under the door a little tighter," he'd added, sniffing the hallway.

Paulie introduced everyone. As the only woman in the place, I was bound to attract attention. The most persistent of the bunch was this guy named Wiz. Wiz was cute but had the unfortunate conversational tic of ending every statement with a question: "You know what I'm sayin'?" It took every ounce of self-control to prevent myself from blurting, "No, I don't know what you're sayin', so shut the fuck up already." Wiz was cool so I wasn't about to go there. My time-tested disassociation tactic was as useful as ever. As he talked, I gazed at his face in apparent interest and focused on the music until I'd tuned him out completely.

While Wiz talked, I had the distinct impression someone was watching me with an intense, soul-piercing stare. I traced the gaze to the other side of the room where a guy leaned against the wall with one leg bent up under him. He was dressed in the standard uniform: Timberlands, baggy jeans and a hoodie. His posture was also basic: hood up, shoulders slumped, with both hands wedged inside his front middle pocket. But there was something very unique about this new character. His gaze seemed to take me in whole and his mysterious charisma carried across the room, giving me a charge.

Wiz was still in my grill, but for all I heard he might as well have been miming at me. My attention was on the enigmatic guy across the room. It didn't take long for him to approach.

"What's up? How you doin'. I'm Nas, Nasir."

So this was the mysterious friend of Paulie's that I'd been hearing about. He was of average height and build. He pulled back his hood and I finally got a good look at him. A clear caramel complexion. A baby Afro, fine and curly, the kind you want to run your fingers through. His unique Arabic name suited him—this Nas character seemed to come from another place and time. There was something about this dude I was drawn to.

"Hey, I'm Carm, nice to meet you."

The music had become too loud for conversation. And Nas certainly didn't seem like the kind of guy who would shout to be heard.

"I can barely hear myself think. Let's go into the other room," I suggested.

Nas smiled his assent, revealing a set of lower gold teeth incrusted with red rubies. After relocating into the bedroom, Nas became struck with shyness and fell silent.

"So, where are you from? Where do you live?" Somebody had to get the conversation rolling.

"Queensbridge. You know where that's at?" he mumbled.

"No, not really."

"It's in Long Island City, right before you get on the Fifty-Ninth Street Bridge. It's cool."

"So, what school did you go to?"

"I ain't get to finish school. I dropped out in the eighth grade."

"My mother would've killed me if I hadn't finished school."

Nas started to relax into the conversation. "My moms don't worry much about it. She was too busy working, there was nothing she could really do, you know."

As we continued talking, I could see that Nas was way more than your average run-of-the-mill thug from the projects. He was laid back, quiet and very intriguing. He told me the usual stories about hustling as a teenager, but when he talked he always found an interesting way to say things. He was innately smart, high-IQ smart.

"So, Carm, when we gonna go out?" he asked.

I wanted to take it nice and slow with Nas. "Why don't I bring a friend and we can double, maybe with your brother?"

"My brother's too young. My friend Will was my age, though." His voice was breaking and he paused before he went on. "Will lived in the apartment above me and was like my brother. He was my first DJ. He made the first track I ever spit to."

"Is Will one of the dudes in the living room?" I asked. His demeanor took another shift. "Nah, Will is walking with the gods," he replied.

"What happened to him?" I asked gently.

"Well, Will was messing with this chick and she had a man and when the dude found out that she was cheating on him he came to the projects looking for Will."

As Nas told me the story of how his best friend was murdered, I could see the pain in his eyes.

"When he saw him, he just started bustin' and shot Will in the back. My brother Jabari got hit too, in the leg. Me and my moms were in the crib and when we heard the shots, my moms screamed, 'Jabari,' like she knew my brother got hit."

"That's fucked up." I couldn't imagine losing a best friend. It was obvious that this was still a fresh wound for Nas.

We talked a little more. But if his eyes had seemed a little remote before, they were now absolutely empty. He was off alone, roaming distant deserts of grief. His monologue suddenly stopped.

"Are you okay?"

"Yeah, I'm alright, I just need to get some air. I'll be back in a minute."

An hour passed and Nas still hadn't returned, so I decided to go look for him. It was a freezing cold night and I had no idea where to even begin to look for this boy. When I found him, he was sitting in the park on the back of a bench with his feet on the seat. He was hunched over, elbows on knees, head in hands.

"You okay?"

Nas wiped away his tears when he heard me approaching, but his caramel cheeks were streaked with darker toffee-colored stains.

"Yeah, I'm good."

It was a very personal moment and I didn't want to invade his privacy, but I had to do something so I moved closer to Nas and put my hands on his thighs. With two fingers, I lifted his face up to mine and gave him the ghost of a kiss. Just that faint brush of the lips swelled my heart with feeling.

It was a peculiar but romantic moment. Although I had promised myself that I was going to remain single, I was falling for Nasir Jones.

CHAPTER 2

Growing Pains

· · · · · · · · · ·

I THINK I DEVELOPED my taste in men spending time with my father. As a little girl, I loved going to bars with my father in the late afternoon, when their languor seemed like a miracle. Just outside, traffic rushed by. But inside, there was the tranquility of clinking ice, mellow, natural light and muted conversations. Our visits were never consistent; however, I enjoyed every single moment of Papa Lenny's time and attention. Being with him was always a real treat. When my dad was around, he took me everywhere with him. We didn't participate in typical father/daughter activities like the park or the movies. Papa Lenny was straight hood, not that he was a drug dealer or hustler. He was more like a freelance criminal who simply enjoyed what he did. We did skirmishes on the boulevard, fried chicken wings and French fries at the Chinese restaurant and lots and lots of bars. This afternoon it was The Sir James on Merrick Boulevard in Queens.

"The kid is in the house!" Papa Lenny shouted. Papa Lenny was very intriguing, adventurous, the life of any party—a true ghetto celeb. He always looked good, smelled good and always kept a fresh shape-up.

Everyone in the bar turned to look at me: a seven-year-old in cornrow braids with red and white beads that matched my terry cloth romper. Enthusiastic shouts of love for Papa Lenny and me both. We walked along the bar through thickets of smoke. My father stopped to high-five some men playing cards, painted women nestled up against them. We took a seat in the back.

"Gin and juice, baby," Papa Lenny called up to the barmaid. He smiled over at me. "Bring me two of them."

I went along with his game, since I had no idea what I was drinking. I gagged and spit it out on the table. It was horrible.

"You just had your first drink!" Papa Lenny exclaimed. He laughed and ordered me a Coke.

We paid our respects to the barmaid on our way out. "Bring her back again soon," she said to Papa Lenny. "She's such a cute little thing."

"I'll see you later," Papa Lenny said, laying a long kiss on her. I knew better than to mention our cocktail hour to Sha Sha or I might not see Papa Lenny again for a long time.

My parents met in the second grade in Brooklyn, New York. When my mother turned fourteen, her parents decided to move the family of five to St. Albans, a prominent neighborhood in Jamaica, Queens, with a diverse makeup of blue collar workers, musicians, doctors and lawyers. It was the perfect place to raise a family. After she graduated from college my mother's brief marriage to my brother's father dissolved. Papa Lenny's family coincidentally relocated to the same neighborhood a few years later. Inevitably my parents bumped heads and the reunion soon developed into a loving relationship.

Papa Lenny came from a good and hardworking family; however, he had adapted to a lifestyle that included crime, violence and substance abuse. Sha Sha was oblivious to the fact that my father enjoyed and prided himself on being a freelance criminal. But when the wheels of love are in motion, there are no more rules. After dating for several weeks Sha Sha became pregnant. Although the pregnancy wasn't planned, Sha Sha believed that it was a blessing considering that she was on birth control.

On December 23, two days after I was born, Papa Lenny and his friends arrived at the hospital pissy drunk, reeking of whiskey and cigarette smoke, with the intention of giving us a ride home. Papa Lenny had been celebrating the birth of his only child for the past two days. The truth is, Papa Lenny didn't need an excuse to drink, he was an alcoholic. He and his friends rented a U-Haul and stashed a few wooden chairs and a radio in the back. Needless to say, Sha Sha refused to leave with him and his cronies, so they eventually left. The next day, the same hospital that we had just been discharged from was now calling to inform my grandparents that Papa Lenny had been in a terrible car accident. My father lost two friends and came extremely close to losing his own life. After breaking just about every bone in his body, Papa Lenny went through eighteen months of recovery and rehabilitation. But nothing could put a cap on my dad!

Sha Sha left Papa Lenny when I was four. By this time, his drinking habit had worsened and the physical and mental abuse was entirely unbearable. He had a hard time letting us go and adjusting to life without us, and would often show up at Sha Sha's place of business unannounced and inebriated, and cause a scene. Even then I knew he was just confused about how to love us. Besides, I could never hold a grudge against someone who was so much fun and had so much style. But he was in and out of prison so it was very difficult to keep in touch. Writing and sending my father letters became a weekly ritual. I cherished his return letters, especially the ones with hand-drawn pictures of flowers, clowns and teddy bears.

When Sha Sha left Papa Lenny, we moved in with my grandparents in St. Albans. There was plenty of room for us in their four-bedroom house, which had a huge living room, dining room, full basement and backyard.

It was cool at Grandma's, but like most little girls, I wanted to be with my mother every single moment. It was next to impossible because Sha Sha had two jobs and went to school part-time. Sha Sha is very ambitious, focused and brilliant, not to mention gorgeous, with an hourglass figure that brings traffic to a halt. Aside from playing the piano and violin, Sha Sha also speaks fluent Spanish and could debate any subject, geopolitical or otherwise. I'll never forget switching channels as a teenager and catching my mother in the audience on *The Phil Donahue Show,* asking a question. I was so proud of her, I called her immediately at work, "Mom, Mom . . . I just saw you on *Phil Donahue.*" By the end of the night we must have received over fifty calls. Sha Sha was also very popular.

I didn't see a whole lot of Sha Sha during this period; she worked nights at a bank and went to school full-time. It wasn't always great living with my grandparents, who kept an immaculate and strict household. My brother, Van, even developed a stuttering habit because he was on edge all the time.

Life wasn't exactly peaches and cream at Grandma's but just across the street lived my best friend, Tameika, a slightly chubby girl with a crazy sense of humor who always took my mind off anything negative. We spent almost all our free time together, making mud pies in her backyard, having water fights and playing double Dutch.

By the time I was eight, Sha Sha had worked her way up to a better job and we were able to move into our own apartment in Flushing, Queens, apartment 7C. On Saturdays I took piano and ballet lessons at the Brooklyn Conservatory of Music. Sha Sha tried to compensate for our father's shortcomings with strict parenting and plenty of cultural activities. But we were latchkey kids. When my mother was at work or school, Van and I entertained ourselves by throwing homemade concoctions off the terrace at passersby or racing up and down the hallway to see who was faster. Sometimes we would just beach up in front of the TV for *What's Happening Now!!* or an episode of *Diff'rent Strokes.*

In Flushing I made a new best friend, Felicia, who lived in the building across the street with both of her parents. Felicia and I grew close enough to call each other cousins and her parents,

Imogene and Robert, whom we called "Robit," became more like an aunt and uncle. Imogene and Robert were the coolest parents. They took us everywhere! USA Roller Skating Rink, the movies, the park, the pool, you name it, we were there.

Robert was from Harlem and reminded me so much of Papa Lenny. Papa Lenny had been in and out of jail over the last couple of years. We stayed in contact through letters and brief phone conversations. For a minute, Robert became my surrogate parent, and when it was just us kids and Robert, we'd sneak uptown to the numbers spots in Harlem. Our little secret.

One day while watching cartoons at Felicia's, Robert eyed me critically.

"Carmen, anybody ever teach you how to fight?"

"Yeah, I know how to fight." Of course I didn't, but I couldn't let the cat out of the bag just yet.

"I'm not talking about you and Van play boxing. I'm talking about out on the street, 'ready to go for yours if you had to' fighting."

Felicia and I were fascinated. We were dying to learn something new.

Robert, tugging on one of my cornrow braids, said, "Okay, let's start your first lesson." I involuntarily smiled at his display of affection and looked over at Felicia, who wore her hair just the same as me. "I'm gonna teach ya'll both how to protect yourselves out there," he said.

On weekends, Robert trained us in street fighting techniques, like how to punch a person in the face and sweep her off her feet at the same time. He showed us how to wrestle—most important, how to hold the other girl down. And he gave us the street fighting code that would later lead me on many a crusade for girlfriends in need:

"Felicia, if Carmen is having a fight, then you jump in. And Carmen, if Felicia is having a fight, you jump in. There is no such thing as a fair fight on the street." Felicia and I continued to grow and train as tag team partners and often caused major havoc in the neighborhood. We eventually became bullies, thanks to Robert.

• • •

By the time I turned ten years old, I had learned how to cook, clean, do laundry and the grocery shopping, and take the bus across town to visit my grandparents, which wasn't too often, but as often as Sha Sha would let me. On occasion, Papa Lenny would show up. He had relocated to Chicago and got married. My little sister Janine (Nini) was born a year later. I couldn't wait to be a big sister. In my early teens my aunt Carmen, Sha Sha's younger sister, introduced me to the Black Spectrum Theater on Merrick Boulevard in Jamaica, Queens. Their after-school curriculum gave my natural energy a dramatic focus and lent direction to my creativity. That's when I decided to become an actress or maybe an artist. Vanessa Williams had just been crowned Miss America, so in my mind anything was possible.

At the time I was preparing to go to a zoned high school, which I dreaded. When I found out that Art & Design High School was still accepting applications, I immediately pulled my portfolio together, applied and was accepted.

Design high school opened my eyes to life's bigger picture. I saw that individuality and self-expression could be a way of life, and I loved it.

When school started, I took the train to Manhattan every morning with Sha Sha, who was a professor at Baruch College. Soon, the city was like a second home to me. The first person I met at Art & Design was Richie. Richie was from Brooklyn, Puerto-Rican, super cute, with a low fade and a small build. Richie and I hit it off instantly. We had a few classes together and shared the same lunch period. We would joke around in class, go to the movies, hang out in the Village, you name it. Richie put me onto a world outside of Queens. We even had matching gold teeth and Gucci sneakers. We were the best of friends. Traveling to the big city was definitely an adventure for me. I felt like adulthood was nearing and that I was way more mature than most teens my age. I really thought I was doing it!

I was a late bloomer and nervous about fitting in with the other kids in the city but over the summer things changed for me, physically and otherwise. All my padded bras went into the trash and my jeans started to fit way too snugly. I also learned how to drive. At fifteen I was chauffeuring my uncle Mike and his friends around Queens in his pea green Impala. I was so tiny that I had to sit on a pillow in order to reach the steering wheel, but I caught on quick. As fall drew near, it was time to get serious. So I joined the Suzie Vance Talent Modeling Agency in Forest Hills, Queens.

Modeling wasn't my life's ambition, plus I was only 5'2", but if everyone thought I could, why not give it a chance? The Susie Vance Talent Agency put my portfolio together. When they called with jobs, though, I'd usually be too busy hanging out with my friends.

School was school, but after school, well, that was another story: Tameika and I were getting into more and more trouble. We were still the best of friends and spoke daily, although we lived two bus rides away.

By high school Tameika and I were tight with another girl, Monica, a cute around-the-way type who could do stand-up comedy for real. She was the only person I knew besides Felicia who didn't grow up in a single-parent household. Her three sisters lived with her, too. Going over to Monica's house was like visiting the Huxtables (minus Theo): the rock-solid family foundation, the confidence and comfort of knowing that no matter what happened they would all stick together. *No wonder Monica was so funny,* I'd think. She could afford to be.

Although I loved fashion and modeling I was still an around-the-way girl at heart myself. On occasion Tameika and I would get into physical altercations for whatever reason and we always came prepared. We wore razors in our ponytails "just in case," and kept a jar of Vaseline on us at all times. We weren't looking for trouble, but somehow trouble always found us. It was better to be safe than to be sorry.

On the weekends we reformed for our jobs at Fine Fare, a supermarket on Merrick Boulevard. The part-time work kept me in Guess, Benetton, Nike Uptowns and bamboo earrings. One Saturday while at work I met a cutie-pie named Corey. Excuse me, Corey D. He was more than a few inches taller than I was, with a caramel complexion, a mouth full of gold teeth and a smile you'd die for. He wore a fresh haircut and crisp sneakers. He knew Tameika from the neighborhood and tossed her a nod. Then he turned his attention to me as he approached my register.

"What's ya name, shorty?" he asked.

"Carmen," I replied.

"My name is Corey, Corey D. You want to be my new girlfriend?"

Was he kidding me? "No, I just met you," I replied, rolling my eyes.

He pulled out a big wad of money and paid for his items. After I gave him his change, he said, "You're going to be my girlfriend. Watch!"

He reached over the counter, grabbed the back of my neck and pulled me toward him, pressing his mouth on mine. I pulled away and tried to regain my balance. My manager started yelling and cursing at him in Arabic.

"What the fuck?" I yelled.

Corey just laughed. "I'll be back, Carm."

After my shock wore off, I found myself a little turned on by Corey's cockiness. So we eventually hooked up, but we never became too serious. Corey was a little too wild for me. Every day, it seemed, he was either involved in a shootout, in the emergency room, or arrested on some misdemeanor. He ended up doing a few years in jail for selling drugs. Crack was the newest and hottest fix on the street during this era. By the end of high school, just about everyone I knew either sold crack, had a boyfriend who sold crack or actually was on crack, though you didn't stay in touch with those people for long. In fact, I met two of my best lifelong friends, Danae and Tarja, on the bus to Riker's Island when we were visiting boyfriends there. Danae was very petite and cute with Bette Davis eyes. Tarja was fly! Thin, long hair, pretty face, great body and very stylish. Unlike Tarja and Danae and their significant others, I didn't have a long history with Corey and became bored with the weekly visits. Corey and I still corresponded through letters and a few phone calls, but that was about it. I couldn't be bothered. Plus Corey couldn't squeeze a dime out of me. All of my earnings went to designer clothing and jewelry. Our time together was short but sweet.

To me, news reports on the "alarming crack epidemic in our cities" seemed to be broadcast from a parallel universe. Hustling was a regular job with bigger payoffs than bagging groceries down at Fine Fare. Sure, sometimes violence erupted or jail time was served, but the quick money was worth the risk for guys, and us girls usually stayed out of the real trouble.

Most teenage girls in Queens entertained themselves as I did, hanging at the mall, picking up the latest fashions, getting our hair and nails done. But my free spirit would collide head-on with Sha Sha, who worshipped at the altar of education.

"Ma, why are you so gung ho about college?" I asked Sha Sha. "You wanted to be a violinist, not a professor." My grandparents had more or less forced her into a practical profession, and she'd studied education at Wilbur Force Academy in Ohio instead of music at Juilliard.

"I know, and that's why I have issues now." Sha Sha had an answer for everything. "Carmen, I don't care what you and your brother choose to do in life. You want to be a short-order cook, that's fine, but get a degree in culinary arts first." By the end of high school, I felt like I'd just been released from doing a twelve-year bid. I wasn't about to serve any more time.

"Mom, I'm gonna be a model or an actress or something. I don't need college." "Looks fade, Carmen. An education lasts forever," she said.

I knew that college certainly would distract me from the action and adventure I'd found with my friends. And even more significantly, I saw education as a step on the slippery slope toward having a life without adventure. Sha Sha became so structured because she had to, then somewhere along the way she forgot how to be anything else. Overworking and overextending yourself were for my mother's generation. I had a totally different agenda. It was time to do me and experience and explore the world.

CHAPTER 3

"Ready for the World"

. . . .

IT WAS A YEAR after graduation. Summer had just arrived and I was working at my uncle's law firm, still hanging out with my friends and still searching for a way out of Queens. I spent most of my free time with my best friends Tameika and Monica. Tameika still lived across the street from Grandma's and Monica lived just a few blocks away. The three of us were inseparable.

One day Tameika and I went over to visit our friend Hasan. Hasan and I had been introduced through Monica and we hit it off instantly, though not in a romantic way. In fact we later discovered that we were actually cousins. What a small world.

Hasan wasn't home, but his friend John let us in and introduced us to his friend Troy. He stood close to six feet, with a light brown complexion, medium build and wore the sexiest smile I'd ever seen. He was hot! Troy wore a gray velour Fila sweat suit and gold chains galore.

"So what's your name?" Troy asked, wasting no time.

"Who are you supposed to be, Slick Rick?" I asked.

His coconut Muslim oil scent was having a profound effect on my hormones. He smelled delicious. I was immediately drawn to him, but had to play it cool.

"Niggas like Slick Rick take their fashion tips from me," Troy said.

"Well, where are you from?" I asked.

"I'm from New Haven, Connecticut," Troy said, failing to mention that he was dating Hasan's sister, Marie. "How old are you, Carmen? You legal yet?"

Before I could answer, John stepped in between us. "Um, excuse me, Troy, Marie is on her way. She will be here any minute. Don't play yaself!"

Troy broke out laughing. "What? You better go 'head. This nigga is crazy!"

On that note, Tameika and I bounced. "Tameika, did you see him?" I asked breathlessly on the way home.

"Yes, girl, and he is fine. You better get with him," she counseled.

"What about you know who?"

Tameika simply shrugged her shoulders.

When it was time to ring in the new year, Monica, Tameika and I decided to do it in style at Encore, a club on Jamaica Avenue. At the last minute we couldn't find a sitter for Tameika's one-year-old son, Bryan, whom she'd named after me, so we went with our default strategy. Tameika told her mother she was going to the store, then grabbed the outfit she'd previously stashed by the side door and met us at Monica's house. Tameika's mother was used to it; we pulled this stunt on the regular.

When Tameika arrived, Monica was putting the finishing touches on my hair. Monica was an aspiring hairdresser, and she'd hooked me up with a tightly pulled and heavily gelled ponytail with an attached hairpiece, which she hot-curled and pinned into a bun. My head was killing me by the time Monica finished. The price of beauty. Tameika wore a shoulder-length bob curled at the ends; Monica's hair was in micro braids and pulled up into a ponytail. Their outfits matched my ensemble: tight black leather pants and mustard yellow leather bolero jacket. We made it a policy to dress in sync.

We got plenty of hollers and honks as we walked up to the club. Just in front of the entrance, I noticed a brazenly double-parked red Benz with Connecticut plates. An image of Troy flashed in my mind. Could he be here?

The club was so packed, you could barely move. As we maneuvered our way through the tough crowd, I soon smelled a familiar coconut scent and a few seconds later spotted Troy approaching in a black leather sweatsuit and matching sneakers, looking as good as he had months ago.

"Whatcha doin' in here?" he said, smiling from ear to ear.

"Same as you, celebrating the new year."

I maintained my composure even though my heart threatened to beat its way out of my chest. Oddly enough, Troy moved over and whispered something in Tameika's ear. Tameika smiled and extended her right palm. Troy slapped a $100 bill in it. Tameika whispered something back to him.

Troy then leaned over to whisper in my ear. "I'm going to call you tonight."

"Excuse me?" I replied.

"I knew you weren't gonna give me your number, so I got it from your friend," he said with a laugh.

I looked at Tameika. "You gave him my number?"

"Look, I gotta pay my phone bill," she said defensively. I feigned anger for a minute but was actually flattered.

A few months later, after numerous phone calls and late-night conversations, Troy mentioned he'd be coming to town soon. By this time he and Marie had broken up so it was all good.

One beautiful summer night, the stars were shining extra bright and the breeze was slight, but perfect. Tameika and I were sitting on her front stoop.

"Did he call you back yet?" Tameika inquired.

"Yes and no. He called, asked for my address but then got right off the phone. What does that mean?" I asked worriedly.

"He probably has a girlfriend in New York and he went to go check her first."

As soon as Tameika finished her sentence a red Benz pulled up. It was him, Troy Johnson. That explained why he'd asked for my address, so he could sneak up on me. Troy pulled up to the curb, music blasting, slouching over into the passenger side with one hand not so much holding the steering wheel as caressing it. Something about him reminded me of Corey D. Maybe it was his casual and cocky demeanor, which said: "What? I ain't from around here and I'm by myself." After all, he didn't know if I had a boyfriend or not! He was fearless and I loved that. A man with confidence is a sure turn-on.

As I walked over to meet him, he sat reclined in the driver's seat, watching my every step, so I made sure to add a little extra sass to my already seductive walk. My hair was in a curly ponytail and I wore cut-off jean shorts with a T-shirt knotted in the back and a pair of Stan Smith Adidas.

"What are you doing here?" By this time I was nervous as hell.

"I was in the neighborhood," he said. Pretty sure!

For the next hour or so, Troy and I talked about everything under the sun. I could literally feel myself melting before his eyes. I must admit, Troy had that effect on me. I was very, very curious and wanted to know more about him. I could tell he was out there as far as the women were concerned, but I was still interested. If nothing more, he would be a challenge. The only question was whether he had a girl. Tameika may have hit it right on the nose after all. He never questioned my status or mentioned his. Now I knew there was no way in the world that this dude did not have some kind of girl waiting for him. But then again, that was not going to be the focus of my immediate attention.

"You want to go for a ride?" Troy asked.

"Sure," I said.

The next thing I knew we were on our way to New Haven, Connecticut. We pulled into town about an hour and a half later. As soon as Troy stepped out of the car, it all came together for me.

Everybody on the block swarmed around us, as if Troy were the Messiah returning home from a pilgrimage. This was his block, he was the king of Hurbert Street. I mean, don't get me wrong—from the minute we met I knew exactly what he was into, I just had no idea to what degree. Now, I had dated little so-called drug dealers from around my way in the past, but this was different. Troy was on another level.

"Who dat, Troy?"

"Man, she blazin'!" rang from all directions.

"This is Carmen, my new girlfriend. She's from New York. Now ya'll niggas back up and stop sweating her."

I'm thinking, *New girlfriend?*

It was getting late and Troy was ready to go. "Come on, let's get ghost."

I wasn't used to the lingo, but caught on quickly.

Fifteen minutes later we pulled into the Comfort Inn. Troy kept a room there so he didn't always have to be at his parents' house. We ordered room service and talked the entire night. I don't remember what time I passed out but when I woke up, Troy was nestled behind me, his arm wrapped around my waist. He was a gentleman after all.

For the next few days, Troy took me everywhere. The more people he introduced me to, the more information I absorbed. Troy was a complete package; undoubtably manly and exactly what I desired. His ghetto fabulous lifestyle afforded him celebrity status in a miniscule town. Everyone from the local cab drivers, the fiends, the police, down to the gas station attendants knew Troy Johnson in some way, shape or form. He was definitely the wild card in the deck and secured his boulevard business with an iron fist. Yet instinct told me that there was another side to him, one that was tender and caring; but in order to preserve his reputation in the streets he often hid his true nature.

Troy worked with his cousin Casual, one of the few people he trusted. Casual was pretty low-key and functioned as the brains of their operation. Casual's frame had a 6'2" stretch, a firm build and soft mocha brown skin. They were players on the same team and you rarely saw one without the other. I was having the time of my life in New Haven! I was so intrigued by my new surroundings that I completely lost track of time. Before I knew it a whole week had passed and I still hadn't called home. I knew if I called, Sha Sha would let me have it, even though I had made arrangements for Monica to fill in for me at my uncle's law firm. No use spoiling my impromptu vacation.

Troy sprung for new clothes, et cetera, so I really didn't want for anything. Our typical day consisted of sleeping in late, grabbing a bite to eat and collecting profits from his handlers by any means necessary. By nightfall we were watching movies and getting high. I was definitely feeling him and it was obvious that the feeling was mutual.

When I finally returned home, Sha Sha was livid, and who could blame her? "You're so grown, but too scared to call me and tell me you went out of town. You want me to treat you like an adult, Carmen, then act like one."

Oy vey! What else could I say? I knew I was wrong and apologized over and over again. When things calmed down, I headed back to New Haven, this time letting Sha Sha know I'd be spending the weekend away with friends.

Troy and I grew closer over the next couple of months, and he asked me to move to New Haven. I was a little astonished, however I accepted just as quickly as he'd asked. *Why not?* I thought. *What do I have to lose?*

To accept his invitation was one thing, but to act on it, well, that was another story altogether. Sha Sha would never condone such ridiculousness. Convincing my mother to allow me to relocate to another state was going to be tricky. I would have to devise a plan that would appeal to Sha Sha's interests and concerns. After a day of strategic planning, I announced that I was going to college after all; in New Haven, Connecticut. There was still a fifty-fifty chance that Sha Sha would go for it. And she did! She actually thought going to school in another state was a good prospect. As long as I was in school, Sha Sha was supportive. Besides, she was totally against any career that involved the entertainment business. Once again I had come up with the ideal plan.

New Haven, Connecticut, get ready—'cause here I come!

* * *

My plan was moving along very well. Sha Sha helped me to secure a nice, quaint apartment on the north side of town, far from Hurbert Street, but not too far. You see, my mother just had to be a part of the whole process—after all, this was her dream come true. At least she was sending one of her kids off to college. I failed to mention the "community" part—oh well. After I got settled, Sha Sha returned to the city. My first day in my brand-new apartment couldn't have felt better. I finally had my own place and the sense of independence that I so longed for. That was, until I received a disturbing phone call from Casual, Troy's cousin.

Apparently, Troy had been arrested. What else was new? But his rap sheet was about a mile long, so it was evident that Troy was going to have to do some time. I couldn't believe it. What a hard pill to swallow. Would this be the final chapter to my summer love fling? What the hell was I going to do now? This new situation threw a monkey wrench in my master plan. I couldn't just pick up and retreat. I had already registered for classes. I surely wasn't planning on filling out any fast-food restaurant applications. Not! I had to think quickly.

To make ends meet, most people worked two and three part-time jobs and hustled on the side. I honestly couldn't complain, because Casual always looked out for me. I guess that was his way of looking out for Troy. At the time I was jobless and it was becoming extremely difficult to pay the bills. Eventually I landed a part-time gig as a nail technician. Don't ask me how, but I managed to skate through the interview. I certainly wasn't qualified for the position, but figured hey, I've been getting my nails done for years, I should be able to pull it off. I was hired on the spot. Not only did I have a new job, but I also inherited a new pet. On my walk home, I stumbled across a stray orange-and-white-striped kitten. He couldn't have been more than six weeks old and was the cutest and littlest thing. Without a second thought, I took him home, cleaned him up and named him Nathan. Now I had two men in my life. Although Nathan kept me company, I missed Troy and visited him as often as I could. Casual came by to check on me from time to time. He struggled to hold down the business in Troy's absence.

It was a late Friday evening when Paul and Casual stopped by for a visit. We hung out for what seemed like hours, laughing, joking, just shooting the breeze. Casual had a heavy burden to unload and casually talked about the drug game. Despite the increasing drug epidemic that plagued New Haven, Casual still could never seem to break a thousand dollars a day and his street dominance was on the wane.

"The block ain't pumpin' like it used to," Casual complained that night, his six-foot frame stretched all the way across my couch. We'd popped a bottle of Alize and were doing it some damage. "Shit is dead! It looks like a desert out there. Where the fuck did all the coke fiends go?"

"Coke? All this time I thought y'all were selling crack," I said carelessly.

"Yeah, there are some little niggas from the projects that tried to sling crack," Casual said. "Barely made enough to re-up. But then again, they probably didn't know what they were doing."

Casual had a new glow in his eyes. You would have thought that he hit the number! Crack was the solution to all his troubles. His only problem was where to begin his fresh new start and how. Viewing Casual in this new light was rather awkward. By the time we crashed in my living room, it was near dawn.

That following Monday I was up early preparing for work when I heard a knock at my front door. "Who could that be this early?" I thought. It was Casual, and he had company. "Carm, this is Mary. Mary, this is Carm, the young lady I was telling you about."

Mary was a West Indian woman who spoke with a thick Jamaican accent. Her appearance was a bit startling to say the least. I remember thinking, *What rock did she just crawl from under?* She appeared to be in her late thirties, about 5'5", 160 pounds, brown-skinned, with extremely large breasts. Mary sported a stained T-shirt, raggedy denim shorts, head scarf and slippers. She was also missing several teeth. Before I could say a word, she just shoved right past me and bogarted her way into my apartment. After wandering through my apartment room by room, she turned to Casual and snickered. "Bumba Ras, you don't sleep over, right?"

I later learned that Mary was inquisitive by nature. Casual replied coyly, making it clear that he and I were just friends. Mary was a handful. She was far from shy and spoke her mind. Meanwhile I was in complete disarray. "Who is this woman and why is she here?" Casual explained that he was in a tight spot and could use my help. He had it all worked out. Mary's sole purpose was to transform coke into crack. The only missing piece to the puzzle was a location.

"Oh, hell no. You want to use my apartment?" I barked.

"Carm, please, you think I would be here if I had another spot? You're the only one that can help me and that I trust," he pleaded.

"Pretty sure," I said.

But, it wasn't long before I was convinced. Casual promised to pay my rent, all my bills, provide transportation and hit me off with cash. He also explained how this was just a temporary situation, just until Mary got her new place.

The following week, Casual and his tactless new protégée arrived according to schedule. Mary seemed quite anxious and immediately set up shop in the kitchen. My humble abode was turning into a drug lab right before my eyes.

First, Mary opened a big red cooler and pulled out the tools of her mad science: a scale, glass cooking vials, wax bags and a china white brick of coke. I couldn't believe this was happening in my apartment.

Casual and I observed closely as she put the cocaine in a glass vial, adding water and a pinch or two of baking soda. Holding the mixture over a flame, she stirred it a little. It all happened so quickly. Then she poured it onto a plate. In a few seconds the liquid had hardened into a white cookie. She chopped it up into little pieces and put them in several wax bags. Mary named the product "Cook 'em Up," nice and simple.

We all looked at each other, wondering who would try it first. They knew I sure wasn't going to smoke that shit. Mary, however, didn't hesitate to light up the rock. The smell was too much for me and I escaped into the bathroom.

Minutes later Mary was lurching around the apartment, singing, dancing and telling jokes. She started calling out Casual about how she was underpaid for her services. "Ya mon, I have two kids to support!" Before long she was making no sense at all. She stopped talking and manically cleaned my apartment from top to bottom.

Yes, by all appearances Casual's crack concoction was indeed marketable and ready for distribution. He was soon in business as the Nino Brown of New Haven, and his block was back on top. Hurbert Street went from making $900 to $9,000 a day. Whenever Mary came in with that cooler, I knew they would be pulling an all-nighter. The long hours and hard work finally paid off. Hurbert Street was back on the map.

Casual and I spent many hours together, bagging up, exchanging our life stories, our dreams and fears. The attraction was mutual, though I guess we were both afraid of making the first move. Mary would constantly ask us if anything was going on, but we both denied having any kind of relationship outside of business. It was the truth. However, the truth changed as it always does. Before I knew it, I ended up in a relationship with Casual as well as with Troy—if you can call it a relationship when one of the parties is locked up.

• • •

Casual continued to reign supreme and I continued to play my part and keep up with my daily visits to the correctional facility. Money was longer, the summer seemed hotter and everyone Casual had on payroll enjoyed the fruits of their labor.

Even though the money was pouring in and I was having the time of my life, I still wasn't content with my new lifestyle. I was very much aware of the fact that I was operating a crack den in my kitchen, and all this could lead to time behind bars. Not to mention the emotional battle of being caught between my two lovers. It was time to take a break from the overwhelming tension and visit home, so I went to visit my friend Monica. Even though Monica and I were very close, I could never tell her, or anyone for that matter, what I was doing in Connecticut.

During my short stay at Monica's, I recharged and when it was time for me to go back, I didn't think twice about inviting her back to New Haven for the short weekend. We never did business on Sundays, so Monica would never find out about the operation. Imagine my shock and horror when we walked in to see Casual and Mary working at the kitchen table. They were apparently working overtime, in flagrant disregard of my house rules! I was pissed. But I really couldn't beef the way I wanted to. Casual had a key and he paid my rent and bills.

"Where have you been and who's that with you?" Casual asked with the craziest look on his face. "That's my friend Monica, from New York. Is that a problem?" I didn't appreciate his harsh questioning. "What the hell are you two doing in my apartment on a Sunday?"

Monica looked around, scoping the evidence on the table. "What the fuck?"

Deadly silence took over. Casual and Mary quickly put away their equipment and left. They knew a straight arrow when they saw one.

After their abrupt departure, Monica continued her tirade. "Bitch, are you crazy? Carm, do you know what comes with this type of lifestyle? Do you know the trouble you'll be in if the feds run up in here? Not to mention the bitches calling and knocking on your door wanting to fight you. And what about your career? What are you doing?"

Monica was preaching like Sha Sha during one of her parental sermons. I felt like I was twelve again, busted and embarassed. Just like with Sha Sha I had to tune Monica out for a second. I knew exactly what I was doing and didn't need to be schooled or checked by Monica. I had already been doing that for a minute now.

"Oh, Monica, please! Don't try to sit up here and act like you're some little Miss Goody Two-Shoes," I snapped.

"Do you like him? Did you sleep with him?" Monica went on.

"And don't try and change the subject either, but the answer to your question is, yes to both."

It actually felt great to finally just let the truth out. "I think I love him, Monica. Even if he already has a girlfriend and a baby mother."

"Of course he does." She rolled her eyes. "What about Troy? That nigga you moved up here for? Carmen, are you crazy?"

"I love him, too. Maybe I am crazy." And it was the truth. I still had feelings for Troy. Now I was also in love with Casual. Sometimes I'd try to choose between them, but I would always rebel against that difficult decision. Whoever said we were genetically predisposed to have feelings for only one person at a time anyway?

Before Monica got on the train the next day, she swore to keep my life in New Haven a secret. Monica's heart was always in the right place, and though she may have been a little angry and disappointed, she was still my girl and never passed judgment. I was a little disappointed in myself, too, which was probably why I'd kept my new lifestyle a secret from my old friends.

Mentally I was fatigued, but way more in tune with my innermost feelings. It was time to have an open dialogue with Casual and tell him how I felt. After dropping Monica at the train station, I took a ride to Hurbert Street in search of Casual. When I rolled up, the block resembled a ghost town. It was completely void of any signs of life; not even a fiend was seen walking the street. I felt like I had just stepped into the twilight zone.

A local store owner informed me that the block had been

swept in a concrete raid courtesy of the New Haven police department. Everyone was arrested, but I couldn't get confirmation on Casual. Just in case, I had to move quickly. But I obviously wasn't moving fast enough. The moment I stepped out onto the pavement, I was snatched, handcuffed and tossed in the back of a police car. My charge was disturbing the peace. *You gotta be fucking kidding me!* I thought. Who was I disturbing? There wasn't a human being in sight. It was my first run-in with the law. Thank God this wasn't Queens! Total embarrassment.

Waiting in that dirty decrepit cell was worse than sitting in the police car, which in itself was a humiliating experience. But nothing could be worse than the thought of Sha Sha being called to New Haven if the authorities discovered the red cooler in my apartment. It was her name that was on the lease.

"Holy shit, Sha Sha." Even though I wouldn't hear the end of it, I knew that I could depend on my mother for anything, including bailing me out of jail. Fortunately, that wasn't necessary. I was released a few hours later and given a warning. All I wanted to do was go home, take a bath and wait for Casual to call.

Hours later, I was awakened by Casual's key turning the lock to my front door. He was barely inside when I noticed something was wrong.

"Casual, what's the matter? Are you okay?"

After failing to pull himself together, Casual broke down and collapsed on the sofa. *Are those tears?* I asked myself.

It was clear that Casual had been in a recent altercation. His white T-shirt was stained and ripped, his knuckles were raw and covered with blood.

"I'm alright, Carm. I'm just tired of the bullshit. I'm tired of these fake, jealous niggas, these wack-ass bitches, I'm just tired of every-fucking-body. I'm ready to quit this shit and go back to school and do something different with my life." This made me realize that even the most masculine of men are not immune to having sensitive emotions. That's when I made the decision that I wanted to be with Casual. I'd tell him I was breaking up with Troy so we could really be together. Then I'd move on fixing the rest.

I had yet to talk to Troy, but I was able to relocate the operation when Mary finally moved into her new apartment just a few blocks from Hurbert Street. The place was a dump but offered shelter. Mary couldn't have been more thrilled. Casual refused to come inside and ended up dropping me off. Over the past year, Mary and I had become close friends. She was the only "real" person in New Haven that I trusted. Our friendship was misunderstood by most. I loved hanging out with Mary, she reminded me of Papa Lenny in a sense. Mary was loud like my father, opinionated like my father and most of all, she loved to have a good time and make people laugh, just like my father. I didn't judge her and accepted her for who she was.

One night, Mary insisted that a friend of hers drive me home. She had male company and Casual was caught up. On the ride home, I noticed flashing police lights in the rearview mirror signaling us to pull over, but the driver ignored the request. "Are you crazy, pull over."

"I can't. I got warrants."

Just my luck. I thought as I secured my seat belt.

The chase was on. My heart was beating as loud as the sirens, which were roaring fiercely. As we maneuvered our way in and out of traffic and up a one-way alley the dissolving police lights gave the driver hope that he might just pull it off. I looked back and saw there was no way they'd catch up to us. I couldn't believe what was happening. It was just like being on the big screen. When the coast was clear, we hopped out of the car, over a fence and entered a small ranch-style house through the back door. The homeowners were friends of the driver and let me call a cab. I was pissed, but played it cool. I just wanted to get the fuck out of there and quick-fast.

A couple of days later my super showed up at my door to give me the heads-up. The feds had visited the rental office and asked questions about my mother, as the apartment was in her name. That night I lay awake, my mind spinning anxiously with questions. How did my life get to this point? I put the last year on rewind and carefully re-examined it in slow motion. I knew it was time for a change.

But first I needed to head over to the correctional facility to see Troy. These visits had become lackluster for me, though I was relieved Troy was still clueless about my romance with Casual.

During the visit we talked about my trip home to Queens. My eyes kept straying down to my watch as I checked to see if our allotted visiting period was up. You'd have thought I was the one doing time. Finally the visit was over. As I was rushing out of the holding area, a young woman with a little girl walked up to the security desk.

"I'm here to see Troy Johnson," she said.

I stopped and stared. This must be his girlfriend and daughter, the family he'd assured me was out of the picture. *Well,* I thought wryly, *there's no need to have Troy called down for their visit.* He was still in the holding area where I had just left him.

I came right out and asked her. "Are you here to see Troy?"

She didn't say a word at first. Then she sighed, "Here we go again." I could tell by the look in her eyes that she had been down this road many times before.

I thought, *Is this what I have to look forward to?* It was clear, Troy and I had no future. I just turned around and walked away. That was the last time I saw Troy. I would no longer make trips back and forth to the detention center for a man who had a girlfriend doing the same thing.

The very next morning, I rented a U-Haul and stashed it up the street. The day skated by as I stuck to my normal routine. I stopped by Paul's for a quick visit and had a feeling that he knew I was leaving town and for good. Luckily I didn't bump into Casual. Our split left me feeling very emotional, not to mention vulnerable.

That night I pulled the U-Haul up to my front door and tossed in all of my belongings. I took one last drive down Hurbert Street, saying farewell to my New Haven life, and hit the highway.

The drive to New York was more like a mental roller coaster ride. I loved Troy and what Casual and I shared was very special, but when you are dealing with any drug dealer the reality is that rough edge and baller mentality that makes you so attracted to them is the same rough edge and baller mentality that won't allow them to settle down with just you! That is why they are called hustlers. It's a lifestyle and women come with it. The game ended for me on my stretch down I-95. I realized that not only was change inevitable but very necessary. As I put the pedal to the metal, I thanked God for all of my experiences and the ones to come and never looked back.

CHAPTER 4

Turning Over a New Leaf

· · · · · · · · · ·

I ARRIVED AT VAN and Paulie's a few hours later. After unpacking, I called Nas to inform him I was in town permanently. He was ecstatic and we made plans to hook up as soon as I was settled. My first priority was to find a means of support—it was time to provide for myself. The rent was only five hundred dollars and would now be split three ways, but even that small sum was a lot of money for someone without a job. Luckily Paulie knew of a part-time position available at a place called Rush Management.

"Where?" I had never heard of the company.

Paulie had recently signed on as a producer there. "Russell Simmons's management company for music producers."

I had no clue what it would be like to work in the entertainment industry. I imagined a stuffy, buttoned-down environment:

white men in dark suits with furrowed brows walking anxiously down brightly lit halls. Well, I could use the connects for my aspiring career in show biz, which had stalled during my year in New Haven. And anything would beat what I was doing, which was absolutely nothing. This could be perfect, actually.

Two weeks later, I had a job at Rush Management. Not in a corporate midtown office as I'd imagined, but in a narrow, three-story brick building down on Elizabeth Street, just on the edge of Little Italy. The office atmosphere was loud and colorful but relaxed, a little like the African drumming circles down in Prospect Park on weekends. Even when things got busy at Rush and Def Jam, everyone stayed cool. Paulie's manager, Linda Burke, was my boss. Linda reminded me of my aunt Carmen, laid back and all natural with dreads and beautifully glowing skin. Like everyone else, she dressed casually. Her office had muted lighting and smelled of the essential oils she wore. But there was no nonsense in Linda's approach to business. I could definitely thrive working for her.

The music business was very new to me. I had no idea what I was really in for. The hustle and bustle of it all was quite exhilarating. *I landed the perfect job,* I thought.

Russell Simmons himself was rarely at the office. The H.N.I.C. was Lyor Cohen, a tall white guy with dark curly hair and skater sneakers. The first one at the office in the morning and the last to leave at night, he too was a pleasure to work with. He was always cordial; however, everyone knew his limits. He was rather kind to all of the women in the office, but the men—that was another story.

I did have one slight problem. Almost every time I transferred a call to Lyor, it would come right back. His office was so busy, his assistants rarely picked up the phone. Once, I worried it might actually cost me my job.

It was one of those hectic afternoons when Run DMC, ONYX, and a few other Def Jam artists were all heading out on the road. The phones were going crazy. No matter how hard I worked to keep up with the calls, Lyor's office was jamming up the lines good. Lots of bounced-back callers got angry, but one guy became absolutely irate. "Why the fuck can't I get through to this office!" he raged. He sounded like a self-important artist who thought he could flex on the new receptionist.

"Join the crowd!" I blasted back. "You think you're the only one trying to get through? You can either tell me who it is you want to speak to or come up here and help us answer these damn phones."

"This is Russell, Russell Simmons, the owner of those damn phones." His voice had lowered to a mere bark. "Just put me through to Lyor."

Oops. My job flashed before my eyes. I put him through. As usual, the call came back.

"What the hell is going on there?" Russell asked.

"Russell, Lyor's office isn't picking up calls," I confessed.

Russell arrived ten minutes later, dashing by with a brief hello on his way up to Lyor's office. I don't know what Russell said, but Lyor's office was much more responsive after that day.

For most of us, Rush was a family-style, close-knit operation. My first day on the job I met an intern, Rennette, who'd grown up in the same circles I had in Queens. Rennette was very pretty with a glowing complexion and a dancer's sinewy strength. Over the years I'd learn she had a heart of gold as well. People like Rennette made going to work so much fun that I'd often look at my watch and realize my workday had officially been over for an hour.

Rush's security guard, Monster, discouraged trouble from artists most of the time. He was actually the sweetest man you'd ever meet, but his 6'6", 400-pound frame sent out a different message.

I absolutely loved my new job! So did my girlfriends. Every chance they got, they would make unannounced visits; frequents ones at that. I knew the real reason they were dropping by. They only hoped to "bump" into a rapper or entertainer, anyone who'd been in the limelight. The transformation would be so counterfeit. The tone of my friends' voices would suddenly change from that of an around-the-way girl tone to a soft, demure, sweet and plastic one. The wardrobe was a whole other story: short miniskirts and midriff tops that left nothing to the imagination. Their exposed skin glistened with sparkling lotion that they applied ten times before getting off the elevator. It was all topped off by heavy makeup that MAC intended for nighttime. This was who they were and I was fine with it. All I could do was sit back and laugh. Linda didn't mind the visits as long as it didn't interfere with my work and it never did. I was convinced I had the coolest boss in the world.

Soon after I settled in at home and work, Nas and I went on our first official date. Neither of us had a car, so we took a cab to a local movie theater. We saw *Malcolm X*, starring Denzel Washington in a scary good performance as the man himself and Angela Bassett as his wife, Betty. As we watched the movie, I could feel Nas staring at me, but when I glanced back at him, he'd quickly turn his head. After the movie we decided to go back to my house and grabbed a cab.

"You believe in love at first sight?" I asked.

"Why, you in love with me?" he teased.

"No . . . but there's something about you that I love already."

He smiled. "I feel the same way you do."

I had a sudden urge to take care of him. I wanted him to be my partner. We talked about how his parents had gotten married after only knowing each other for six months. Anything was possible. We held hands, moved in closer and kissed all the way home, except for a quick stop at the liquor store for a bottle of Alize.

When we arrived home, Nas and I popped the bottle of Alize and got cozy on the couch while we smoked a blunt.

"So what did you do today?" I asked.

"Nothing much, I just hung out in the projects and chilled at my mom's crib, nothing much."

The funny thing about Nas was he seemed like he was never in the studio. Now that I worked in the industry I knew a record deal didn't necessarily mean anything. It certainly didn't guarantee success. You needed a hit. Although Nas wasn't focused, it was so refreshing to be with someone who at least had plans beyond that night. It inspired me to tell him about my own plans.

"So, I just finished a photo shoot, for BAMN, that urban

clothing line. The designers were seeking fresh new faces. Mine fit the bill."

Nas changed the subject, which should have told me something. But I barely noticed his disinterest in my career, because the Alize and weed were working their magic. We started kissing and were quickly all over each other like wrestlers. Nas became a human octopus, simultaneously touching my breasts, my thighs, and my butt. Although I wanted him just as much as he wanted me, I had to slow things down. We ended the night wrapped in each other's arms, watching a movie.

• • •

From that night on, Nas and I spent every free moment together. Of course money was scarce. His advance from the Columbia deal was long gone by the time we met. When you're newly in love, though, your form of recreation is irrelevant, so we happily did a lot of free stuff: leisurely walks in the park, picnics, endless hours browsing bookstores and the movies.

As our intellectual and spiritual connection strengthened, so did our physical attraction. Nas was avidly affectionate. He would stroke my cheek and softly kiss my neck until I was ready to surrender to anything. That's when I'd suddenly find his hand down my shirt. I'd allow him a quick feel here and there but always shut him down before things got too heavy. It was only a matter of time until the inevitable, I realized, but I wanted to prolong the sweet torture of foreplay.

A couple of weeks later, Van and Paulie moved to an apartment in the building across the street. They were building a studio and needed the extra space. The privacy was just what Nas and I needed. Our first night alone, I cooked dinner and we smoked. Nas looked very comfortable and relaxed as he slouched beside me on the couch. He wore his stoned face: chinky, slanted eyes and relaxed jaw. Turned out he wasn't as tranquil as he looked. When we began to kiss, he tried to get slick and unfastened my bra. I went with it this time. My bra came off and all my clothes followed right behind. Before I knew it, Nas and I were completely naked. His manhood stood erect. His size was average, but that didn't diminish my desire to jump on him.

We just stared at each other for a long moment. It felt like everything in our lives had led up to this point when I would bend over to kiss him, his lips so inviting, wet, and juicy, and those lips would later work miracles on hidden parts of my body. He nudged my body down, inch by inch, slowly, slowly, until I sat perfectly on top of him.

As soon as I was centered, Nas immediately started thrusting inside of me. I told him to be still, then took my time riding him. After a few minutes, Nas picked me up and carried me into the bedroom. Our gentle lovemaking turned into pure, hot, passionate sex. Afterward we lay in each other's arms, naked and silent. A few minutes later, Nas proposed.

"Carm, let's get married."

I was shocked. "Really? You want to get married?"

"Yeah, I mean my moms and my pops got married after only knowing each other for six months."

We talked all night about our future wedding and eventually fell off to sleep.

As the weeks passed our courtship bloomed as did our friendship. Nas would often surprise me at work with flowers and candy. We also partied together. We'd get drunk beyond belief, go home and have sex all night. Sex in the morning, sex in the evening, sex in closets. We were having the time of our lives and couldn't get enough of each other.

• • •

It had been two months and I couldn't have been happier with Nas. He was everything I desired in a man and a partner. He was thoughtful, kind, and considerate of my every need. I could feel that this relationship was going to be long-term. Things couldn't have been going better. Then something completely unexpected threw me for a loop. The mirror confirmed that I looked as bad as I felt. My face was pale and there were bags under my eyes; I looked like a raccoon! The weight of my limbs was enough to drag me back down to bed. Stomach-churning nausea made putting anything in my mouth a liability, even my toothbrush. What the hell was going on? I looked over at Nas, baby-faced with sleep. I had to pull it together and catch the subway to work. Slowly, slowly, I left the bathroom to get dressed. One step out the door, I puked all over myself. Tameika. She'd be awake already. I called her. Before I'd described half my symptoms she blurted, "You're pregnant!"

Nas and I had just started dating. There was no way we could have a baby this early in the relationship. But my conscience recoiled at the prospect of having an abortion. Later that evening I broke the news to Nas. He was apprehensive and uncertain but never said a word to articulate his feelings. He didn't need to. Neither of us was ready to have a baby.

The waiting area at the clinic was crowded. Although every woman sitting in that waiting area was unique, with different stories, we all shared one thing in common: We were all terminating living beings. It was harsh but true. I sat down and filled out the necessary paperwork and returned it to the front desk. Nothing to do but wait. Some girls came with their boyfriends, some didn't. Nas sat next to me placidly reading a book. I was so nervous. I glanced around the room. There was a young girl who had just come in, probably about thirteen, with a little girl's face and huge belly. She looked like she was about four months along. I stopped myself. There was no use worrying about just how pregnant she was.

Finally a nurse called my name. I kissed Nas and proceeded through the white double doors. Hours later it was over and I left with birth control pills and a painful, unforgettable memory.

When a couple makes the decision about whether or not to have a baby, they make a family decision. Even if they don't keep the baby, they become family to each other. An abortion forces a couple to discuss difficult feelings that might otherwise take months or years to reveal. Nas and I became even closer very quickly. So I wasn't too surprised when soon after the procedure Nas showed up at my door one evening with a large duffel bag.

"I need to get out of the projects for a while. Is it alright if I stay with you for about a week?" he asked. Even though he hadn't yet finished his album, he explained, some people in the neighborhood were already jealous. "Shit is getting crazy."

A week passed. Then two weeks. By the end of the month Nas was still living with me. I didn't know if he even looked around for another option and I didn't care. I wanted him to stay. While I went to work, Nas stayed home or occasionally went to the studio. I came home and cooked every night and happily catered to his every need. We were perfectly content.

My girlfriends, however, weren't too thrilled about my new boyfriend. "He's just using you, girl! He doesn't even have a car, no money and he's not contributing to any of your bills."

"Don't worry about what I'm doing," I'd say. "Nas is doing the best he can to finish his album. I don't care if he's focused or not, I'll stand behind him one hundred percent."

Most important, we were in love! My friends acted like they couldn't understand the kind of love Nas and I shared, even though their situations were no better. Everything was perfect as far I was concerned. So perfect, in fact, that I neglected to take my birth control pills regularly. But I didn't worry about practicalities. Fretting about protection was for unfortunate people whose lovemaking lacked profundity, I thought. Three months later I was pregnant again. Nas was emphatic when I gave him the news. "Carm, I want you to keep the baby."

Like him I was still in mourning over the last abortion, but I was just settling into my work and was unprepared for a child financially or emotionally. It was only our fourth month together and though everything was going strong, it couldn't hurt for our relationship to grow to another level before we had a child. I was devastated and an emotional wreck. I couldn't believe this happened again. I thought I had been careful but obviously not careful enough. I had always wanted to be a parent and I finally found the perfect person to share it with, but I knew we were too young to take on this type of responsibility.

We talked it over and made the difficult decision to abort again.

"Promise me this," Nas said. "If there's a next time, we'll keep the baby."

It was late at night by the time we'd decided how to handle the pregnancy. We needed to go out and get some air. A walk to the store would do us both good. On the way, we bumped into Black, a neighborhood friend of mine.

"What's up, Carm," he called as he walked toward us.

"Hey, Black," I answered.

Nas copped an attitude and ice-grilled him as we passed. But Nas didn't even know Black. Where was this aggression coming from?

"Damn, nigga, I know her. I was just saying hi," Black insisted.

I had had enough and went into the store. By the time I came out, Black was being loaded onto the back of an ambulance. I didn't know what happened, and I didn't even want to know. Nas's naked insecurity was offensive on every level. I could only guess that due to the emotional ordeal that we had experienced, Nas was feeling very possessive. We went right home and tried to forget the incident. Unfortunately news of the confrontation spread and the phone began to ring. It would continue all night long.

I was sick with worry that Black might retaliate. A vengeful visit still seemed imminent the next morning when we got a call from Sha Sha. The rental office claimed they had received numerous complaints about a tenant living in the apartment who was not on the lease. The "real" was they wanted us out so they could double the rent.

There was nothing Sha Sha could do. Nas suggested we stay with his mother on a temporary basis. Nas and I had to be together and this seemed like the only way. Next stop, Queensbridge!

CHAPTER 5

The Bridge

· · · · · · · · · ·

I WAS OFFICIALLY A resident of Queensbridge. Although I had
been to Nas's mother's house many times, I didn't know what
to expect from actually living in the projects. Nas first took me
to Queensbridge the morning after he proposed. I'd liked Mrs.
Jones at first sight. Her warm personality made visits to her home
a pleasure. She had a golden skin, a full, round face and a youth-
ful smile. My first visit there, she made glazed ham, candied
yams, collard greens and buttermilk biscuits. And the woman's
cooking was a force to be reckoned with.

On that first visit, we walked up to a typical scene in the courtyard. There was a small six-inch TV perched on a vinyl chair with
a ripped seat, foam poking out in places. The set was powered by
an extension cord that snaked all the way down from an apartment on the third floor. Two guys in their late teens were sitting

on a bench in front of the TV battling it out on a Playstation like they were in their living room.

"That is so ghetto!" I said.

"Where they supposed to play, Carm?"

"If they can go to all that trouble to juice up their Playstation, they can go get a job and get their own place."

"Whatever, Carm. This is the Bridge, take it or leave it," Nas replied.

We moved our things over to Mrs. Jones's two-bedroom apartment on the 41st Street side of the Bridge. She opened her home to us with southern hospitality and treated me like family. Mrs. Jones also relished the chance to keep a watchful eye on her son. But limited space made our living arrangements very awkward. Jabari, Nas's younger brother, gave us his room. Jabari was lean with piercing eyes and displayed much of his stress on his face. Believe me, it frequently broadcast strain after we moved in and he was exiled to the couch. It was hard to be grateful to Jabari for his sacrifice: his room was just a 9 x 9 box with only one small window. A single twin bed and three-drawer dresser accented the limited space. There was little ventilation, and the room was hot and moist in the summer, a veritable Turkish bath. It was quite tense. One day Nas and Jabari went to blows when Jabari continued to voice his displeasure regarding us living there. Nas swung first, catching Jabari in the nose. It was a tie and they both lost!

A few days after I moved in, my friend Rennette came over to visit. She stopped short at the door. "Carm, this is a pigsty! Nas and Jabari were total slobs. How can you live here?" It was just she and I in the apartment, so she was free to speak her mind.

Rennette cleared away newspapers, bills and dirty dishes to make space for her purse on the dining room table. She looked over to the living room. "And it looks like somebody took a razor to the couch," she said.

"That's exactly what happened. Nas told me he was watching his neighbor's son and took a nap. When he woke up the couch looked like somebody took a machete to it."

"Well, I have to clean this house. I can't take it."

"Believe me, I know how you feel. But it's beyond cleaning. They need a whole new apartment."

"C'mon, let's start with the kitchen." Rennette marched purposefully over to the sink. She turned around holding a dripping, stained tube sock on the end of a fork. "Don't tell me this is their dishrag," she sneered, wrinkling her nose.

"Mmmn-hmm. Why don't you peek inside the freezer?" The roach carcass frozen in ice made an even bigger impression on her. It was a wrap for Rennette's cleaning project.

"You're right, it's too much," she admitted.

I eventually did resort to house cleaning, just to keep myself occupied in the evenings. At first I tried hanging with Nas and his friends after work. The move back to QB was good for Nas, in a way. When we were forced to move back in with his mother, it signified to his friends that maybe there was no money, maybe he was really just a struggling artist, just one of them, despite his Columbia Records affiliation.

When I came down after work one night, they'd been there

all day, debating like a street congress. Regular life in the projects guaranteed especially good gossip. Every night there was juicy news. That particular night it was the story of a friend who was shot in the leg and died instantly. I took a seat on a bench next to Nas. "Hey, boo," he said, kissing me. Everyone nodded hello in my direction and a typical Queensbridge conversation continued. I tried to take an interest, but it all ran together.

"I gonna get this money . . . That nigga soft . . . He coming home from lockdown next week. . . ."

Same old shit. "I'm going to go up and rest a little," I said, excusing myself. I went upstairs, changed into one of Nas's T-shirts and sat up reading in bed.

Nas came up a few minutes later. "Why did you leave so fast?"

"Because y'all are worse than a bunch of women when it comes to gossiping," I teased. The truth was I could not be bothered. Nas's friends couldn't spell *conversation,* let alone have a decent one. "I feel a little strange living here. Mrs. Jones already feels like I'm stealing you away from her. It's like she's the wife and you're the husband and Jabari's the kid. I'm the mistress who disrupts the family." It was one of those insecurities you give voice to in the hope that someone will refute it. Unfortunately, Nas confirmed it.

"My moms just doesn't get you, Carm. You get things done, pulling yourself together every day for office work, meeting new people, and taking care of what you gotta take care of. I'm her son, you know how mothers are.

"You forget I have a brother. Sha Sha's not like that, why should your mother be?" Sha Sha couldn't wait for Van to find a girlfriend and do him.

"You know I love you, boo, don't let it bother you," Nas said, slipping his hands under my T-shirt. "You're perfect. How'd I get so lucky to find a tiny girl with a big butt?"

His hands felt so good on me. "But what about your mother?" I whispered. It was an empty protest, I was already sliding down onto my back. We made love as quietly as we could.

• • •

With all the gloom in the projects, any departure from the everyday routine brought excitement to Queensbridge. See, QB is not really a project. It's a city unto itself, a microcosm. And because people are so packed together there, gossip is as good as having something printed in the paper. So the whole place was buzzing months later when news broke that Mobb Deep would film the video for "Shook Ones Pt. II" in Queensbridge and Puffy was going to make a camco appearance.

When Puff showed up for his part in Mobb Deep's video, you'd have thought the president of the United States had arrived. Little kids, fiends, storeowners, even grandparents all flocked down to the set. Everyone tried to stay visible, hoping to get a little shine from the spotlight fixed on Puffy. The crowd was buzzing with excitement.

"This is some bullshit," Nas said.

I couldn't believe how pissed he was. Nas was livid that Puffy was getting such a reception from his hood. I looked at it much differently. I saw a community united. This was one of the few times when people weren't outside trying to kill one another. It took the filming of a video to give us a positive vision of the place. It was a golden, peaceful day in Queensbridge. Of course, soon everybody was back to ducking for cover.

CHAPTER 6

Music Biz

. . . .

IT WAS LATE MORNING at the 21st-Queensbridge subway stop. Once again the train was late and I was still standing on the platform after 30 minutes. I didn't mind though. Going to work was an escape from the projects and its mentality. I found it frustrating and exhausting to deal with—the pissy broken elevators, the sporadic late-night gunfire, the fiends, the fights, the roaches.

The train came just as my hair was starting to frizz. The frigid air in the car put an end to that. I found a seat and checked my watch. Even with the slow train I'd be early for work, as usual. My long hours at Rush Management gave me refuge from Queensbridge. And it didn't hurt to demonstrate my work ethic to the office management.

That particular afternoon my diligence paid off. Def Jam chief financial officer Marianne Drummond called me into her office to discuss a new full-time position that had opened up in the finance department. She had noticed that I was always early and stayed late without any complaints.

"And more importantly," she added, "everyone in the office just loves you. You have a wonderful personality and you are just what the finance department is looking for."

The new position included a pay raise and my own office. My job was to make sure that the staff and all vendors were paid on time. This responsibility brought me into contact with more Def Jam employees and artists. I was cool with everyone but had my favorites, like Nikki D. Nikki was a little rough around the edges, but at heart she was extremely sweet. Like everyone else at Def Jam, she thought Nas and I were the cutest couple ever.

And Redman, now he was my nigga! The first time he came in to pick up his check, he leaned over, a little scruffy, and slid me a bag of trees. "For you," he said. From that moment we were friends. It was strictly platonic, no flirting—he was cool with Nas, after all. Reggie came to the office with good energy and good jokes.

After his visits, I'd secure my little package way down in the bottom of my purse. I was paranoid that someone would smell it.

There were soon bigger things to worry about at work. One afternoon, I was in my office going over a few accounts when I heard something that sounded like a gunshot. I literally couldn't believe my ears. There was another shot, then another. Definitely gunfire. I jumped up, locked my office door and turned off the light. The space under my desk made a good hiding place. *Oh shit, they are in here shooting! What the fuck?* Then again, this was Def Jam.

Shortly after the shooting I heard my co-workers yelling and scurrying about. It seemed safe to come out, so I went to check on my boss.

"Marianne, are you okay?" I asked.

"I'm just a little shaken up," Marianne said. "I guess everyone is. How about you, will you be all right, Carm?"

A little gunfire wasn't enough to rattle me, but at work I figured I ought to play the role. "Oh, my God, I was soooo scared!" I squealed, in my best impression of bourgeois dismay.

The office was buzzing with rumors. Although I didn't see it, people claimed a group at the very end of a hot streak had a beef with Lyor, alleging Def Jam owed them money. After several failed attempts to get in touch with Lyor, they decided to come up to the office. Apparently, an argument ensued and one of the members pulled out a gun. Of course no one would ever know the real story of what had actually happened. Shortly after the incident, Lyor announced over the intercom that the office was officially closed for the rest of the day.

On my train ride home, I laughed at the performance I'd put on for Marianne. Oh well, just another day at Def Jam. But at least no matter what happened there, I could leave it behind at the end of the day. That wasn't the case at home in Queensbridge.

As soon as I walked in the door, I told Nas what happened, which proved to be a big mistake. "Carm, when are you going to quit that ghetto fucking job?" Nas hated the fact that my job required me to be in the presence of entertainers of any sort. It made him insecure. The shoot-out only added fuel to the fire. But I figured one shoot-out at Def Jam didn't compare to the daily shoot-outs at home. Def Jam was our way out of the projects—I had to work.

But months later nothing had changed. Our living situation was stalling my momentum and diminishing my motivation. Most weekends I stayed with Sha Sha and my grandparents in Jamaica. Sha Sha's tirade would begin as soon as I walked through the door. "How can you stand it over there? Y'all need to find a place fast. I don't like you living in them projects."

Sha Sha was a firm advocate of self-improvement and couldn't stand to see her only daughter backtracking in life. Her aversion to Queensbridge was deep-rooted: Way back when, we lived in the projects for a year. I was in kindergarten and my father had just left the scene. Life in the Redfern Houses in Far Rockaway, Queens, seemed great to Van and me. We shared a huge room and could make all the noise we wanted without getting yelled at. But even then I suspected Sha Sha felt differently about living there. On weekends we escaped to Harlem, where we visited black-owned bookstores and ate at soul food restaurants. Museums, cultural events and children's workshops rounded out the rest of our free time. For all these distractions, at the end of the day it was always back home to Redfern. Sha Sha would tighten her grip on my hand as we entered the building, carefully ignoring the harassment from the lowlifes who hung out in front. When a neighbor's son was shot and killed, there was no more rationalizing our living situation. Sha Sha shuttled us back to our grandparents' house.

"I'm working on the living situation," I told Sha Sha.

She was suspicious. "Are you paying rent over there, are you contributing your share to the household?"

"Mrs. Jones refuses to take my rent money. I do buy groceries." I was saving most of my money.

Some weekends Nas and I took a train ride to visit his musician father, Olu Dara. Olu had all but abandoned Nas when he was in grade school. Olu was a little sanctimonious and would dole out advice like an old sage. During one visit he discussed dating and relationships.

"Until a person is married, they should be free to see and date who they want," Olu said. His resemblance to Nas was uncanny: he possessed the same caramel complexion and sharp features. Olu was a little taller than Nas, though, which gave his words a paternal edge. He looked at both of us and spoke emphatically. "The only time two people are obligated to be committed is when they are married. Goes for a man or a woman. In other words if you're not married, it's cool to do your thing."

Nas nodded in agreement. Even when married, Olu was unfaithful. According to Mrs. Jones, she had told me plenty about Olu and his women, the rootless lifestyle that ruined their marriage and family. "Probably ruined other families, too," she'd add wryly. She said she had always suspected that Olu fathered other women's children while they were married.

While Olu talked, Nas continued nodding heartily, like he was testifying to some biblical truth. Watching him, I remembered another truism: "The apple doesn't fall too far from the tree." Little did Nas know, he would live to embody that theory.

• • •

That October, I woke up feeling nauseous one morning. When the nausea returned the following morning as well, I was pretty sure of the cause. I told Nas I might be pregnant. His face lit up and he ran out excitedly to buy a home pregnancy kit. We stood together nervously over the kit and waited for the pink lines to appear in the window. Positive results! We were so happy. We had made a promise after the last abortion: This time we were keeping the baby.

"Can I tell you something?" Nas confessed. "I got you pregnant on purpose, so we could be bonded for life. I just can't lose you. Ever."

Some women may have felt trapped by his maneuver. Believe me, I'd later question his motives. But at the time I thought it was romantic. Nas would do anything in his power to ensure we stayed together! We celebrated at Sylvia's soul food restaurant in Harlem with Nas's friend AZ and AZ's girlfriend. AZ was also an aspiring rapper and they had collaborated on a song for Nas's debut album, "Life's a Bitch." Nas ordered a bottle of champagne.

"To life, love, happiness and my daughter on the way," he toasted.

"Cheers. Too bad I can only have a sip!" I laughed.

"How do you know it's a girl?" AZ asked.

"We both just have a feeling," I said.

The only hard part would be telling our parents, particularly Sha Sha, who wouldn't likely see the romance in my pregnancy. Our home phone was disconnected, so we went down to the phone booth to call Sha Sha. Nas broke the news while I leaned close and placed my ear near the receiver, straining to hear her response. By the time he handed me the phone, my heart was stuck in my throat. My "hello" came out as a whimper.

"I want to talk to you later in private." Sha Sha's voice was smooth and stern. "Make sure you call me at work first thing in the morning. We're going to have a long talk."

Mrs. Jones, on the other hand, laughed in disbelief when she heard the news. "Are y'all serious? What do the two of you know about having a baby?" She paused, quickly recovering. "Well, I've always wanted a little girl. I hope it's a girl!" From that moment on, Mrs. Jones was on cloud nine while awaiting the baby's arrival.

I waited until the next weekend to talk to Sha Sha, sparing myself the inevitable "You're too young to have a baby" speech. When I finally arrived at Grandma's, she and Sha Sha solemnly guided me over to the kitchen table and sat down across from me. I felt like a disobedient squaw brought before the tribal elders. Sha Sha did the talking.

"Listen, you are grown," she said. "We all know that no matter what advice we give, you are going to do what you want to do regardless. So, all I am saying to you is, if things don't work out with you and Nas, you can always come here. And you and the baby will be taken care of. Don't think for a second that you are stuck!"

Wow! I was expecting a sermon, not this offer of unconditional support. Then I realized why Sha Sha was so prepared to rescue me. She assumed she would have to. After all, my grandparents had to step in when my father wasn't there, giving us a place to stay, taking us to physicals, filling out camp forms.

And before I could stop myself I was remembering that one time. The horrible day when my father showed up at my grandparents' house. My grandparents were out food shopping and Sha Sha wasn't home from work yet. Van and I were playing in the front yard while my aunt Carmen watched us from the stoop. When Papa Lenny got out of the car, I was excited to see him. But I was also confused. He was wobbling as he walked and not making any sense when he talked. You could smell his foul odor from across the yard. My aunt Carmen ran over and grabbed us both. Papa Lenny stumbled over and snatched me by the other arm, catching me off guard.

"These are my kids and I'm taking them with me," he slurred, taking a swing at my aunt Carmen. She fought back as well as she could. I looked around for help as I cried hysterically. In the car, Papa Lenny's friend was slumped over the steering wheel. Why didn't he help us?

Through my tears, I saw a blurred image in the distance. It was Sha Sha running barefoot down the block, holding a shoe in each hand! Sha Sha swung a shoe at Papa Lenny. Hard. He was too drunk to see it coming, and she got him right in the forehead with her heel. A nail sticking out of the heel punctured him, leaving a tiny hole with blood surfacing at the skin. Papa Lenny collapsed.

Sha Sha ran over to the driver, pulled his head off the steering wheel and honked the horn. My father's friend woke up, oblivious to the drama.

"Take Lenny and get the fuck off my block!" she screamed. He dragged my father over to the car, threw him in the backseat and drove away.

Later that night I was awakened by a loud crash. I peeked out in the living room and saw a brick on the floor, broken glass under the window. Papa Lenny had come back. Sha Sha cried and hid her head in the palm of her hands . . . my grandparents screamed out the broken window. The pressure was on and Sha Sha was catching it from all angles. My brother Van had nestled beside me.

"We gone have to move again," he whispered.

• • •

I shook off the bad memories and looked confidently at Sha Sha and Grandma. "Nas and I are in love." I said proudly. "We both have every intention of being a family forever."

• • •

Sha Sha took Nas and me to IHOP for a brunch celebration. Over blueberry pancakes Nas and I chatted happily about our baby on the way.

"Sha Sha, did I tell you what we're gonna name her? It was Nas's idea."

"How do you know it's a girl?" Sha Sha asked.

"We just do," Nas said.

Sha Sha joined in the conversation but didn't quite give herself over to our exuberance. I could sense she still lacked confidence in Nas. He must have sensed it too, because his cheerful talk gradually died away until he finally put down his fork and stared at his plate in silence. Sitting there awkwardly, his face still round with baby fat, he looked much younger than his twenty years.

"Mrs. Sharon, I just want to let you know that, no matter what happens, I will never be the kind of man my father was," he said. His eyes blazed with sincerity. "If something was to happen with me and Carm, I will always take care of my daughter no matter what."

Sha Sha seemed unmoved by his speech.

"We shall see," she said.

CHAPTER 7

Destiny

. . . .

A BRAND-NEW START in a lovely and humble abode; Nas and I had finally moved into our new garden apartment. I was getting closer and closer to my due date and it was time to move. A couple weekends of apartment hunting with Sha Sha turned up a place in Coram, Long Island. It was a beautiful, family-oriented community an hour from the city. Sha Sha insisted on calling it a "hamlet." The apartment had one huge bedroom, a living room, dining room and a balcony. Simple but luxurious. I had saved most of my earnings while living with Mrs. Jones, so that took care of the deposit for our new home. Nas and I moved in on the first of November.

Soon after we moved, Nas's publishing deal finally went through, bringing in enough money for furniture. We splurged on a jade-green leather sofa set, black marble dining room set, and most important, on items for the little one. Sha Sha even let us borrow her red Nissan Sentra. We worked to set up the new place and daydreamed about becoming parents.

My two-hour commute was a bit of a hassle and Def Jam wasn't the haven it had once been. People like Redman were bright counterparts to the office gloom. Our friendship would last for many years and when I eventually moved to California, Reggie and I had many an adventure. The most hilarious of them all would be the time we did bad 'shrooms. Risa, a friend of Danae and Tarja's, was in town on business so we stopped by Reggie's hotel room at the Nico for a quick visit and the next thing I know Risa and Reggie were eating mushrooms and I tried one. At first it was cool but then Reggie and I both started tripping out. Risa's reaction was quite the opposite. I felt like I was dying and she was just as giddy as ever. Reggie ended the night in the emergency room. How I made it home safely is still unknown.

By Thanksgiving, morale at Def Jam was at an all-time low. I planned a company Thanksgiving dinner, hoping to restore our spirits and reestablish a sense of family in the office. Nini, the longtime receptionist, and I put together a menu and asked everyone to bring a dish. We transformed the main conference room into an elegant dining room: a cornucopia centerpiece dressed up the table. We all ate, laughed, drank and had a ball, with Lyor at one end of the table and Def Jam president David Harleston at the other end.

"This was a great idea, Carm," Lyor said.

"Thanks, the pleasure was all mine."

"So how are you feeling?" Lyor's girlfriend was pregnant as

well, so he was especially thoughtful about checking in on my health.

"I'm fine," I said.

"And Nas, how's he coming along with that new record?" Lyor asked. "It's . . . still coming along."

By then I was used to people being all hot and bothered about Nas's debut album. Sometimes it seemed all of New York City was in a fever of anticipation. Everyone assumed perfectionism was delaying Nas's album. Though I hated to admit it, in my view, Nas was simply relaxed to the point of apathy about going into the studio. When we were living in Queensbridge, I'd get calls from Faith Newman, Nas's A&R at Columbia.

"Please get him in the studio, Carm."

Although there was a huge air of excitement hovering over Nas, he really wasn't focused. I supported Nas's career, but it was not on my priority list. I was focused on being a new mother.

. . .

Nas and I got into a regular routine. I left the house every morning at seven o'clock and returned at nine. On days when Nas wasn't in the studio, he had dinner prepared by the time I got home from work.

One night I came home really exhausted. "What's for dinner?" I joked.

"What you think?" Nas asked. It was almost always fried chicken, corn and rice, his favorite meal. "You getting big, how many pounds have you gained, boo?"

"About ten already, somewhere around there. Why, do I look

bad? Do I look fat?" I had become very sensitive in my pregnant state and every little thing felt like a criticism.

"No, boo, you look good, you look great. I like a little extra meat on your bones."

After dinner we would sit and watch TV and he would lean down and rest his head on my stomach and talk to our baby.

"Hey, baby girl. What are you doing in there?"

I felt something like butterflies fluttering in my stomach.

"Nas, I feel something. I think Destiny already knows you."

"Of course she does." He leaned over and put his ear up against my stomach, smiling up at me. Those eyes of his. Before I got pregnant, I'd felt like even if I could swim in Nas's eyes, I wouldn't be close enough to him. Now I had a part of him inside of me, and my affection for him was even stronger and more solid.

• • •

By February my long hours at Def Jam were taking their toll on me. One night I headed home after a particularly strenuous day. By the time a train finally came, the platform was packed and everyone seemed to crowd into the same car I did. Available seats were out of the question; there was barely any standing room. Many people stared at my swollen belly, but no one offered me a seat. I tried to squeeze into a sliver of a space between an oversized woman and a pole. The nice woman tried to scoot over but couldn't do much to accommodate me—her large girth consumed two seats. Better to just stand. As the minutes passed anxiety overwhelmed me. Was there no air at all on this train? I made eye contact with a man standing next to me and grabbed his arm.

"I feel like I'm going to faint," I said. My head was spinning.

"Don't worry, I've got you," he answered.

I must have passed out because when I woke up I was stretched out in the back of an ambulance on my way to the hospital, where I was treated for exhaustion.

After the fainting spell, Nas insisted that I quit my job. "No more Def Jam, Carm, this is it. That job is not worth it. Not only are you risking your health, but the baby's health, too."

A part of me knew that my job and the commute were starting to take its toll, but the reality was I couldn't quit.

"Nas, we need this job, so I can't quit."

He sucked his teeth and gave his usual reply. "Whatever, Carm."

It was still too early in my pregnancy to go on maternity leave without a doctor's order. After a few days off, I went back to work. A week later, I passed out on the train again. This time my doctor agreed I needed a leave of absence. With his note, I could go on a paid hiatus.

Def Jam wasn't too thrilled. I was the only one in the office who'd been trained on our new software, so I continued to work from home, taking calls in bed for a week or two. The ringing telephone irritated Nas, but it eventually subsided. I was able to rest and in a few days, I'd recovered some of my usual vibrancy. Nas remained concerned about my health and wouldn't let me out of his sight. Every time I tried to step out of the room I got a line of questioning from Nas.

"Where are you going now?"

"To the bathroom, do you mind?" I said, lumbering off in that direction.

I wasn't in there thirty seconds before Nas shouted in. "Carm, you all right in there?"

"Yes, Nas, I'm on the damn toilet."

By March, my seventh month, I was huge, thirty-seven pounds heavier. I was all baby. My breasts were heavy as melons and my nipples were sensitive to the slightest touch. That baby couldn't come soon enough.

As I grew closer to my due date, Nas's debut album was also nearing completion. The studio became my home away from home. Nas took me with him everywhere, to photo and video shoots, interviews and publicity meetings. I already knew a lot about the music industry from working at a record label. Now I got an even less glamorous view of the game from the artist's perspective. Photo shoots could be long and exhausting with the wardrobe changes, hot lights, awkward poses and last-minute location changes.

Nas would generously cancel whatever he had scheduled when I was too tired to go out with him. On those days he smoked his trees religiously, a sure sign the pregnancy was taking a toll on him as well. In those final months I became very agitated. I couldn't help it, pregnancy was all so new to me. I was huge, feeling unsexy and fat, not too mention the mood swings, and I mean horrible ones. I was a total bitch for the most part. Poor Nas!

• • •

By mid-June I was two weeks overdue. By now, I was not just expecting the delivery, but demanding it. One afternoon, I had a strange soreness in my vagina, as if it were expanding. I called Sha Sha, who rushed over and advised me to call my doctor.

"Would you like to have your baby today? I can induce your labor this evening."

Sha Sha bursted out with excitement, "Yes, we are having this baby today!" Okay, did Sha Sha just say "we"?

As soon as I hung up the phone, I grabbed my overnight bag and left for the hospital. Nas was out somewhere in the projects, so I called Rennette, who was dating Wiz at the time. Wiz was usually within range of Nas and would hopefully pass along word of the delivery.

Sha Sha and I headed to Beth Israel hospital in Manhattan. The time had finally come. I felt like I had been pregnant for years and couldn't wait to deliver.

After getting settled I was struck with an overwhelming feeling of excitement. After thinking about the process, I suddenly began to panic. *Oh shit, this baby is going to rip right through my vagina any minute now,* I thought. I called for Sha Sha, who was so nervous that I don't think she even realized that she was constantly repeating herself and pacing the room.

"What? What?" Sha Sha asked.

"Mom, I changed my mind, I don't want to have the baby tonight. Tell the nurse that we're going to come back tomorrow." I was a wreck.

"Carmen, Carmen, calm, calm down," she said soothingly.

Nas showed up shortly after, looking lost and nervous. Sha Sha was worn out and was suffering from a migraine headache. She finally left after my doctor arrived. Of course she left him with a few of her own instructions. I took a deep breath and the procedure began.

Even through my most crazed, pain-dazed ranting, Nas held my hand and tried to soothe me. But the process got a little too real for Nas when the doctor cut me in order to prevent the baby from tearing my skin. He couldn't stomach it and flew into the bathroom to vomit.

"It happens all the time," the doctor said. "He'll be fine. Now you keep pushing!"

Minutes later, Destiny Najae Jones arrived in the world, wailing at the top of her lungs. It was June 15, 1994. When the nurse laid Destiny on my chest, I was in complete awe. Nas and I both cried with joy in those first few minutes of her new life. Then the nurses took Destiny to be cleaned up.

Nas watched them mistrustfully. "What are you doing to my Nana?" He already had a nickname for her. "Why is she crying?" he asked repeatedly. The nurses ignored his inquiries and continued to bathe her.

When they brought her back to us, she looked so peaceful, wrapped tightly in her receiving blanket. My little girl, my princess, my blessing and our child! This day would forever change our lives. Nas and I were officially parents!

CHAPTER 8

Parenthood

· · · · · · · · · ·

PARENTHOOD WAS VERY EXCITING, like a whole new beginning. A few days prior, Nas and I were a couple. Now we were a family. What a difference a day makes.

For the week following Destiny's birth, we didn't leave the apartment. The apocalypse itself would have been dull viewing compared to little Destiny. I even watched her sleep to make sure that she was still breathing. Sha Sha visited frequently to make sure that I was eating and getting proper rest. I was breast-feeding, so it was very important that I take care of myself. Destiny was always hungry. I couldn't tell if she was getting enough to eat or if she was just being greedy. For the first time I was living, thinking, and doing for someone other than myself. Surprisingly, it was a relief.

Though Nas loved Destiny as much as I did, he was afraid to touch her. He thought she was too delicate for him and was worried that he would hurt her. He would hold her for only a short while and then give her back to me. Nas's daily routine remained more or less the same, but my days of hanging out until the break of dawn with my friends and sleeping in were over. My whole life had to be readjusted. Already, I couldn't imagine life without Destiny. She had become my whole world.

A couple of weeks later, we took Destiny to Queensbridge to meet Mrs. Jones for the first time. Mrs. Jones worked full-time and lacked transportation, and as a result couldn't visit as frequently as she desired. When I came through the door Mrs. Jones came running over to me and snatched Destiny right out of my arms and started to cry. I had never seen Mrs. Jones so happy. And behind Jabari's weak smile, I could see a huge grin trying to break through. We all knew he was happy to be an uncle. Jabari and I didn't get along at all. I guess he was just extra protective over Nas. However, that day was a beautiful day in the Jones household.

Later that night, Nas was feeling a little frisky. I was truly exhausted and hadn't had my six-week postpartum checkup, when we'd find out if intercourse was safe again.

"Six weeks means six weeks," I said.

"Let me just put the head in, just for a minute," Nas implored. "I swear I just need to feel you for one minute and then I will take it out."

I gave in. He penetrated me and one minute turned into

two. Soon I felt a throbbing pain in my pelvic area. "I knew we should have waited!" I yelled, as angry with myself as I was with Nas. I took some Tylenol and soaked in the tub for a while. That didn't work. An ice pack between my legs didn't help either.

Nas was helpless to relieve my pain. "I'm sorry, boo," he kept repeating. "You alright?"

"This is all your fault! Don't even think about touching me for at least another two weeks."

"Then we'll just have to improvise," he said with a raised eyebrow at this exciting prospect.

"Not tonight. I am in too much pain. Try your luck tomorrow." I turned over and eventually fell asleep. The next morning my body was back to normal and everything was fine.

• • •

A few weeks later, *Illmatic* dropped. Nas performed here and there but stayed close to New York because he didn't want to be away from his new family for long, but it was time for Nas to get on the road and meet his new fans.

Before Nas left for tour, life couldn't have been better. In fact it was great! I had a beautiful daughter, Nas's career was on the rise and I was enjoying motherhood. We decided to take a family trip to the Poconos.

We stayed in a bungalow-style suite with a private entrance. The room had a king-size bed, a heart-shaped Jacuzzi and a private mini pool. Nas brought the weed and we took full advantage of all the perks. For three days, we bonded as a family when

Destiny was awake and Nas and I reunited as lovers while she slept. Our final night in the Poconos, Nas approached me with a sheepish grin.

"Can I take some naked pictures of you?"

I put a hand on my hip and stuck out my chin. "Only on one condition. If I can take some of you, too."

Neither of us knew how to pose in the nude but we enjoyed ourselves trying. A few days later, we got the pictures back and had a good laugh—we both looked so ridiculous. By then it was time for Nas to hit the road.

Illmatic was in full swing at this point. Over the next two weeks Nas was running around like a chicken with its head cut off, preparing for his first tour. He was a little frazzled attempting to put things in order. He had to come up with a concept for the show, figure out who he was bringing on the road with him, decide who was getting paid what and all of the things that come along with touring. Nas had a lot on his plate. I was very supportive of the situation. I didn't beef with him about being away for so long; I knew he had to do what he had to do. And even when Nas would snap at me for no reason, I would let it slide, knowing he was just stressed out.

"I don't know how I'm going to deal with missing you and Destiny," he said, as glumly as if he were going off to war. It took everything I had not to break down crying as he walked out the door. I hadn't realized how much I had grown attached to Nas over the last year.

• • •

While Nas toured, I played the happy homemaker, staying busy with sewing, knitting, painting and decorating, all of which I had learned from Sha Sha. But more important, Destiny and I finally had the chance to really bond. Waking up every morning with her in the bed next to me brought a smile to my face every single morning.

Family and close friends visited. My girlfriends talked as usual: "Girl, you know how them niggas get down when they are out on the road." I wasn't naïve about the situation but refused to visualize the possibilities. What good would it do me to sit home and stress out about what he was doing? I did not intend to become one of those long-suffering sister-girls.

But when Nas came home from tour I did notice a change as soon as I picked him up from the airport. At first I couldn't quite put my finger on it. He seemed eager enough to settle back into family life.

"Carm, the next time I go on the road I'm taking you and Des with me," he said.

"We'd love to go." But in my heart I knew this was another one of his empty promises. He asked many times for us to go on the road with him but they never came about.

He paused, then came over and hugged me hard. "I missed you so much, boo. So what are you cookin' tonight?" Nas loved a home-cooked meal.

Over dinner, as we chatted about the tour and Destiny, I had the growing feeling something was wrong. As if Nas could read my mind, he turned the tables on me.

"Something's not right," he said.

"What do you mean, Nas?"

"I mean it doesn't feel right in my crib. Did you have any niggas over here while I was gone?"

That's when I realized Nas was cheating on me. It wasn't something I suspected; it was something I knew. Not that I expected faithfulness from Nas. I remembered his nodding agreement with Olu's comment that everyone was free to do what they wanted outside marriage. My feelings at that point pierced a hole in my heart that would get bigger if I allowed it to. Later that week, we stopped by my grandmother's and upon entrance Sha Sha could see that I was drained. I had become so caught up in being a mother that I had no time for myself. I guess I hadn't noticed, but Sha Sha did.

"You look horrible. Are you okay? Ma, look at her." Sha Sha was always very blunt.

"Um . . . hum," Grandma joined in.

They were right, I didn't look so hot. But like I mentioned, my world revolved around Destiny, and the furthest thing from my mind was my appearance.

• • •

One day Nas abruptly announced we were going on vacation to the Bahamas. I wasn't ready to leave Destiny. I couldn't imagine being without her for even ten minutes. Sha Sha agreed it was too early, but my grandmother and Nas insisted I go. I reluctantly agreed. I knew that Destiny would be fine with Sha Sha and Grandma for a week.

Nas and I checked into the same hotel where I once stayed

with Sha Sha and Van on a childhood vacation. We ate, drank and smoked the first few days. After that we enjoyed ourselves snorkeling, jet skiing, gambling. We had long, fanciful discussions about what we wanted for Destiny: nothing short of the world and then some. Halfway through the trip, we both started missing Destiny so much that we returned early.

Back home, Nas began to spend money like it was going out of style. He splurged on the biggest big-screen TV, not to mention all the clothes and jewelry he showered on Destiny and me. He purchased a new gold Lexus SE 300 although he wasn't licensed to drive, which meant I had to do all the driving. It drove me nuts. One time Nas called after being forced to drive himself and he was unlucky enough to get pulled over. Since he had no license he would flash his CD cover at the cop and give him some fancy line about being a star. As much as I hate to say it, it worked every time.

I'm not going to front, it agitated me a little when Nas bought pirate loads of jewelry for his friends—it seemed like Nas bought everyone in the projects a chain or ring.

"Nas, if you don't handle your finances right you'll be broke. It's a risky business. Money isn't always consistent."

"You don't have to worry about me providing for you and Destiny ever, Carm."

Nas usually tuned me out when it came to discussions about finance. After all it was his money, and if he wanted to spend it all on his friends, that was his business as long as he took care of his responsibilities. Still, every time I turned around someone was asking Nas for money—immediate family, distant relatives, friends, associates, friends-turned-cousins and don't forget the new friend of the week. Nas aquired friends quickly, and just about everybody had their hand out. And nine times out of ten, if Nas had it and you needed it, it was a done deal.

Even though Nas had a lot of friends, he was very secretive and protective of our family life. With success came a need for a more secure lifestyle. We had to be selective with the company that we kept; we had a little life to look after.

By summer's end it was time for Destiny's first big outing. My friend Tarja was hosting one of her famous barbeques, a perfect opportunity to show off Destiny to all my friends.

"I know you're not taking my daughter to no party in the hood. It's going to be a bunch of niggas sitting around getting drunk! Are you crazy? What is wrong with ya stupid-ass friends?" Now Nas was raging. "Why would they invite you anyway with a new baby?" Nas could be so extra at times. I ignored him and went to the party. I couldn't wait to show Destiny off.

The company of friends was just what I'd needed. I'd been so caught up in motherhood and playing house with Nas that I forgot to take some time out for myself. What I loved most about my friends was that no matter how much time lapsed between visits or outings, when we did link up, everything always fell back into place.

Of course when I got home, Nas was back in my face. "Who was there? What did you do all night? Were any guys trying to get with you? Did you tell any of them where we live?"

A few days later I received a call from Risa, a friend of Danae and Tarja's. We met at the barbeque. It turned out we had plenty in common. We both grew up in the same part of town, we both had a knack for fashion and we both had daughters. Risa and I became pretty much inseparable. We never argued, rarely disagreed and were always into something. Nas thought Risa was cool, and he hated all my other friends with the exception of Tameika and Tarja. But it was just a matter of time before he would flip on Risa, too.

As the weeks passed, I realized something worse than infidelity had happened while Nas was on tour. He'd had a pure dose of celebrity, undiluted by the stuff of everyday life. It was like living with a complete stranger. By this time his friends and family had placed him so high on a pedestal that he bought into it all. It went to his head, and he was no longer the laid-back, thoughtful and humble person I fell in love with.

Nas developed mood swings and constantly contradicted himself, making promises and then reneging on them. It became more and more difficult to live with him, especially as he gradually distanced himself from me and Destiny. I found myself sobbing on a daily, and became extremely depressed and lonely. And you know misery loves company. Nothing like hopping on the horn with a friend to discuss someone else's misfortunes. Anything to deflect from my own.

At first I thought it was me. Maybe I wasn't balancing my time well enough, so I worked to make things better. But nothing changed. Nas was only concerned about his friends and the industry. When he complained about Destiny's carriage taking up too much room in his trunk, I lost it.

"What you say, nigga? Our daughter's carriage is taking up too much room in your trunk? Nas, I will set this car on *fire!* And won't nobody go nowhere."

Of course he tried to play it off because he felt embarrassed and ashamed. At that point I knew what I had to do. It was time for me to contemplate my next move!

CHAPTER 9

Trouble in Thug Paradise

· · · · · · · · · ·

ONLY A FEW MONTHS after his tour Nas's cash flow had dwin-
dled away to nothing. I needed a job. Luckily, I ran into one of
my former co-workers, Tracey Waples. Tracey's office had been
right across from mine at Def Jam and her vivacious personality
and giving nature always kept things fun and light around the
office. Tracey looked as pretty as ever with her long curly hair,
big bright eyes and light, even complexion. She said she was no
longer at Def Jam but now worked as senior vice president of
A&R at Capital Records.

"Hey, you happen to be looking for work?" she asked. "I could
use a really good assistant."

I hesitated for about half a second. "Hell, yeah!" She hired
me on the spot. I'd start after the New Year. Christmas rolled in
and out and as usual; I decorated and cooked a feast. Money was

tight, so Destiny's first Christmas was modest but filled with lots of love.

Nas wasn't too thrilled about my new job but knew we needed the additional income. And, I argued, the two-hour commute would be too long now that I had Destiny, so I moved in with Grandma and Sha Sha and Nas went back to Queensbridge.

Honestly, I was tired of Nas's bullshit and needed a break. I was looking forward to the separation. And now that I had a job, I could save and get my own apartment. I had always dreamed of having a family, and my overall desire was for Destiny to grow up in a household with both parents. But it didn't look like things were going to work out that way. Nas was too busy doin' Nas. Moving in with Grandma and Sha Sha was a blessing in disguise. I had more help with Destiny than I needed.

Nas visited us at my grandmother's frequently at first, then more sporadically. He would pop up in the wee hours of the morning and pass out on the sofa. Grandma was not having it. So on weekends, we'd pool for a hotel room, just to relax and have some privacy.

But I did make him promise one thing: that he'd attend Destiny's christening. My family and I were planning a private ceremony at my grandmother's house. On the big day Mrs. Jones arrived with two of her cousins, right on schedule. My whole family and several friends showed up. The only one missing was Nas. After making several attempts to reach him, I finally told the pastor to start the ceremony. Destiny looked absolutely adorable in a white satin gown with lace trim. The pastor said a prayer as I held her in my arms. When he gently touched her forehead with the tips of his fingers, Destiny's face went red, her mouth opened and she burst out crying. It was quite a vision, her flushed face contrasting with the fancy gown, illuminating her distress at such a holy moment. "That baby can't wait to get out of that dress," Mrs. Jones said, and we all laughed.

After the ceremony was over and everyone had left, Nas finally showed up. I was pissed.

"Boo, I am so sorry."

"I ain't trying to hear it," I hissed.

"Boo, just listen. My nigga G Rap is in town. I was with him at the studio," Nas explained.

"You should have been here," I insisted.

"He's leaving tomorrow, so I had to check him."

"You mean to tell me that you missed your daughter's christening because you were in the studio with G Rap? You got to be fucking kidding me."

"Carm, I'm sorry."

I was so disgusted I couldn't even listen to him anymore. It was always the same thing with Nas. I was through with his empty apologies.

"I have work in the morning. I'll call you tomorrow, Nas."

• • •

I loved my new job, largely because it felt like a party whenever Tracey stepped into the office. Not that work was to be taken lightly. When it came to business Tracey was serious. She'd already signed Hurricane G and Milkbone. They were the only rap acts on our roster at the time. Tracey made no excuses for herself. She knew she had to hustle five times harder than any man in her position.

Tracey and Sean "Puffy" Combs were the best of friends, so we were comped for most of his Bad Boy events. Living with Sha Sha and Grandma gave me full-time childcare for Destiny, freeing me up to take advantage of the after-work parties. Tracey and I would bring our wardrobes and makeup with us to work. When everyone left the office, we'd get ready, call a car service and hit the spot. Sometimes during my lunch break I'd run to Saks Fifth Avenue to have my makeup done while I sent a messenger out to pick up our event passes. It was all a breeze. Of course I also welcomed the distraction from my home life and the chance to have my own social life apart from Nas.

One evening Puffy invited us to the SOS Lounge to watch a pro basketball game. I invited my friend Lorraine along. She reminded me of Keisha from the group Total: beautiful in the face, thick in the waist. Lorraine was loud, a little sneaky, funny as hell, out to get what she could—and a great partner for adventure.

Puff rented out the entire upper floor of SOS for the affair. There was a huge oblong table in the center of the floor filled with plates of food, bottles of wine, appetizer platters and fruit. Russell Simmons, Veronica Webb and LL Cool J mingled among the crowd.

Lorraine ran off quickly to mingle with the other guests. I ate, drank and had a ball. Tracey came over to say hello and we engaged in our typical girly banter. A few moments later a strange look came over her face. It was like she'd seen a ghost.

"What's wrong?" I asked.

She just stared. I looked in the direction of her gaze and saw Nas entering the room. My whole vibe changed. "Party is over." I was so ready to go. I knew that Nas would be eyeballing me the rest of the evening. He wouldn't cause a scene but I wouldn't be able to enjoy myself with him watching my every move.

I tried to leave quickly but couldn't find Lorraine. Nas soon spotted us and walked over to our table and said hello. Then he leaned over to whisper in my ear: "What the fuck are you doing here?"

I just smiled, avoiding a scene. I was no longer in my comfort zone so why force it? I wasn't much of a basketball fan anyway so I called it an early night.

• • •

When spring arrived, Destiny and I moved out of Grandma's and into our own place. I found a nice quaint townhouse apartment in Fresh Meadows, Queens. It was perfect. As far as I was concerned Nas and I had a non-existent relationship. We were done. It was obvious that Nas was going through something. He always seemed down and usually wore the same clothes a few days in a row. It was as if he had given up. He was helplessly fading before my very eyes.

Work was work, not that we had much of it. At first Nas had no idea that I had my own place. Finally Sha Sha broke down and gave him the number. One hour after a brief phone conversation Nas showed up at my door. He roamed through the apartment, nodding and shaking his head as if his approval mattered. Then he pulled a small gold gift box from his jacket pocket. "I got this for you."

It was a gold heart pendant incrusted with diamonds. It was beautiful. Nas left, then came back with all of his things. Old habits are sure hard to break and I let him stay. One of the new additions he brought to my home was a bronze globe with an eagle on it that he had gotten at a flea market. It was one of the ugliest things I had ever seen and he kept on insisting it be a centerpiece for our coffee table. No matter how many times I would hide it in the closet I would come home to find it right back on the table. I hated that globe and I just couldn't get rid of it.

A few weeks after Nas's return, he was back to just hanging out and doing absolutely nothing. The *Illmatic* money was long gone and he refused to tour again. This caused a major cash flow problem. I was paying all the bills, my own car note and insurance. He just didn't have it. On the weekends I would get up right after Nas came in and Destiny and I would be out. I'd drop her at Grandma's and stay out all night. Most times I wouldn't come home until the next morning, anything to get a reaction. This only added to the beef, which was getting worse with time.

Everything I had ever loved about Nas was gone. We barely even spoke some days. Nas was caught up in the hype and worse, I was caught up in Nas. I had put my dreams on the back burner voluntarily and was now resentful. In my mind, Nas was the distraction. And since it was my apartment, I changed the locks, packed his shit including that ugly-ass globe and set it out on the front porch. Nas had to go. So back to the projects his ass went.

• • •

With Nas gone, I could finally unload. That morning, I blasted the music as I cleaned the entire house. I rid the apartment of all Nas remnants and memorabilia. Mrs. Jones called a few days later. I just knew it was an attempt to reunite Nas and me. Then I sensed uneasiness in her tone. In a nutshell, she was ready to get out of the projects. She had worked at the post office for many years and spent just about every dime on Nas and Jabari. When they were younger, she afforded them the newest and hottest sneakers and gear. They both hustled, but it's not like they had to. Mrs. Jones supported every materialistic habit they had and now she was ready to do her. She explained it would be temporary. When I told Sha Sha that Mrs. Jones would be staying with us, she wasn't too thrilled. She couldn't understand why Nas hadn't purchased a house or condo, something for her.

A few days later, I received a call from Nas at work. He didn't sound like himself.

"What's wrong?" I asked.

"Carm, I'm in jail."

My stomach twisted into knots. Nas had been cruising around the projects with his friends as usual. He was pulled over by the cops, who found an unlicensed handgun in the car. Though everyone in the car was arrested, Nas ended up taking the rap because he was the owner of the vehicle. The arrest was especially worrying because Nas had priors and might end up serving time.

I called Scott Felcher, his attorney, and then Neil Schwartz, his accountant. Finally, I called Papa Lenny for some advice.

"Don't worry, he'll be alright," he said.

"I just keep imagining him in a dirty cell with real criminals."

"This is Nas's first gun charge, right? Okay, so the judge will let him off with probation."

"Are you sure?" I asked.

"Your daddy's an expert on these things, remember?"

"Good question. I'll keep you posted," I said, hanging up the phone. I felt empty inside knowing Nas was locked up. That's when it registered that Nas still had a firm grip on me. Even though he and I weren't on good terms, he was still my daughter's father. Maybe I wasn't empty of all feelings for Nas. I just knew I couldn't bear the thought of him doing time.

The next day Neil Schwartz arrived at the courthouse. Tracey even appeared, ready to pull out her checkbook and put up the bail herself. Just as Papa Lenny predicted, Nas was released on bail and ordered to report to his probation officer. Nas still wasn't going to the studio and was still hanging out all night with his friends, but at least I could breathe again! For some reason Nas just didn't enjoy performing, which meant he rarely booked shows. Good thing I had a job. Additionally a friend of Nas's crashed and totaled his Lexus, so now we were down to one car, mine. *Just great,* I thought. I'd bought a little cream-colored J30. I didn't mind Nas driving my car, but I was concerned because he still didn't have a license. Slowly but surely our relationship began to dissolve once again. Nas's attitude and words became increasingly foul and the tension was thick enough to cut with a knife. While doing some household chores one day I came across a poem that I had written for Nas months back. I found it crumpled up, torn and dusty under the couch. I was so hurt. It was impossible to fight back the stream of tears. I had poured my heart out in that poem and it was obvious that my efforts were in vain. As a result I turned bitter and cold. I had had it. I had even dropped nearly twenty pounds. But as unhappy as I was in my relationship, I was filled with utter joy whenever I laid eyes on Destiny. She was my center, my core, my reason to stay focused. She also had a birthday coming, and I wanted it to be perfect.

Funds were low so Sha Sha and Papa Lenny were kind enough to foot the bill. Destiny's first birthday was a smash. I invited family and a few close friends. Nas invited his friends but none of them brought their kids. Typical!

At the end of the celebration, Mrs. Jones and Jabari's girlfriend Shelly hung around and helped to clean up. I called a few of Nas's friends a cab and soon the house was empty and back to normal. That was, until I received a phone call from the dispatcher at the cab company I had called an hour earlier. Apparently Nas's unruly ghetto friends bailed on the cabdriver without paying the fare. I had to put on the "I don't know what you're talking about" role just to get off the phone. I couldn't believe it. Neither could Mrs. Jones—she was pissed. When I told Nas about the incident, he just nonchalantly brushed it off like everything else. Nas's friends were out to get whatever they could. They were users, but then again he used them as well. Professional security was not in the budget, so they made do. It was a win-win situation.

• • •

I was back at work as usual when, two days before New Year's Eve, Puff called Tracey and asked her to help him plan a New Year's Eve party.

"Puff, are you crazy? New Year's is in two days," she objected.

But there was no denying Puff. The party location was Madame CJ Walker's mansion up the Hudson River in Irvington, New York. She'd become the first black millionaire and had made her fortune selling black hair-care products.

That afternoon we took a car service up to check out the mansion. It was an early Renaissance–style palace, with thirty-two rooms of stained-glass windows, vaulted ceilings with intricate moldings and marble staircases. The party would be concentrated in the gigantic living room and an even larger ballroom just steps away.

Tracey and I got right to work, taking down notes and measurements. With only a few days to pull it together, we couldn't create the lavishness of some of Puffy's more renowned parties, but we did manage a nice theme: a white-and-gold platinum motif for the streamers and balloons, matching invites and a swan ice sculpture for the ballroom centerpiece for a romantic effect. We also furnished the place entirely, bringing in every couch and chair, every wineglass and napkin.

A typical Puffy party ensued. Everybody was there—drug dealers, record executives, groupies, rappers, R&B singers and a few actors. And they all wore their best, even if it was borrowed or stolen.

I intended to bring in the new year with a bang. The attentive butlers aided and abetted my aim: there was always one nearby with another glass of champagne. Before I knew it I was pretty tipsy and decided to hit the dance floor. I was getting my step on when I noticed Puff trying to get my attention, smiling and staring suggestively at me. Well, a little flirting couldn't hurt. I winked at him, then decided to take a breather from the socializing and headed to the ladies' room. Just as I passed the front entrance, in walked Nas and AZ.

"What the hell are you doing here?" Nas asked.

"The same thing you're doing here, bringing in the New Year," I slurred.

"Look at you, Carm," he said. "You should be home with Des. You all drunk and shit."

I rolled my eyes and stumbled off to the lounge, over to one of the sofas. Puff's right-hand man Jay Black came over and crashed down beside me. While we talked Puff took a seat nearby. He motioned for me to come over. I wasn't the type of woman who heeled for a man, but Puff's smile convinced me to take a few steps in his direction.

"So what are you doing after the party?" he asked. "I got a spot in the city. Let's hang out for a little while."

I was definitely curious. Puff was especially sexy in the fluorescent light. But I didn't need any more drama. Nas was enough. I declined politely and went back to the dance floor for the duration of the party.

As I was leaving, I felt someone tap me on my shoulder. It was Puff. "Can I talk to you before you leave?" he asked.

He took my hand and led me into the center of the dark, empty ballroom, where we stopped in the room's only shaft of light. He certainly knew how to orchestrate a love scene. I was too enraptured to pull away, eager to see how the scene would play out. He faced me and his arms encircled my waist, his fingers exploring all the skin exposed by my gray glitter open-back jumpsuit. His first kiss was gentle, a light tap of a kiss. He waited a few seconds to kiss me again, long enough for me to grow eager. With the next kiss his tongue made its way into my mouth. I lost myself for a minute, then snapped out of it, feeling embarrassed, exposed, expecting a director to yell "Cut!" What the hell was I doing?

I ran and got the hell out of there, but my guilt about the kiss trailed me for days. It was still gnawing at me when I returned to the office after the New Year. On my first day back at work, the phone rang early in the morning.

"Good morning, Tracey Waples's office . . . Hey, Puff, Tracey's not in yet, but I'll have her call you as soon as she gets in." I spoke quickly, hoping he would just leave a message and hang up.

"I called to speak to you. What did you tell Tracey?" he asked, then went on without waiting for an answer. "What happened at that party should have stayed between me and you."

"Nothing happened. What are you talking about?" The truth was, I'd felt guilty and told Tracey about the kiss. She and Puff shared a past history. They had once been more than just friends and I didn't want to get in the middle of it. So I played it cool and denied spilling the beans.

"Well, she called me on it. I told her that I might have given you the impression that I was feeling you. I mean after all, we were both drunk and having a good time. I also told her that you were a nice girl and not to fire you, so fuck it, don't worry about it."

"Fire me? Wait, what?" I couldn't believe his condescension. "First of all, this job is not all that serious to me. Second, I enjoy working with Tracey, that's my girl, but I can do without the drama."

"That's why I don't know why you told her all of that."

"All of what?" I was confused and decided to end the conversation. "Well, what's done is done. I'll let her know that you called."

Later that night I was awake reading, wondering when and if Nas would come home. Around 1 A.M., the telephone rang. I answered to a strange voice.

"Nas is at a hotel right now under the name Eric Smith and he's with a chick."

"Who is this?" I demanded. Was this a prank? I was hurt and humiliated. I was home with our child, still feeling guilty about a harmless little kiss with Puffy. Meanwhile this nigga was out with the next chick. It was one thing when I felt sure he was cheating in the abstract. But this was all too real: the fake name, the sneaking off to a hotel room.

"Who is this?" I asked again.

The caller hung up. Guided by intuition I pulled out the Yellow Pages and called every hotel by the airport. I finally found one that had an Eric Smith as a registered guest. Nas answered. When he heard my voice, he hung up. I called back again and again, but he wouldn't answer. I was furious. My heart was racing and my imagination was running wild.

I got Destiny out of bed and drove blindly to the hotel, where they refused to give me any information. The disappointment cleared my head and I went home. What was I thinking, dragging my child out in the middle of the night for a man who obviously didn't want to be home? Heartache spiked with self-loathing kept me awake all night long. The next morning Nas showed up as I was getting ready for work, claiming he had spent the night at Wiz's house in the projects. I knew what he would say so I said nothing. I didn't need to hear his denials and lies. We didn't speak to each other for days.

• • •

But I was good for giving Nas second and third chances. Still I was frustrated cohabiting as strangers in a relationship that barely existed. That's when I met Amar. He was the uncle of my cousin Felicia's son. Amar was cute. He was dark, with a medium build and had a distinguishing mole on his cheek. We hung out, had a few drinks and ended up at his place. By the time I reached home it was daylight. I was still a little tipsy and without scruples and failed to notice the huge hicky on my neck. Nas noticed immediately. The next thing I knew I was being hit in the face with a closed fist. The impact of the blow was so fierce that I saw stars. It all happened so fast. I'm usually quick on my feet, but before I could defend myself or retaliate, Nas was already out the door. The entire right half of my face turned red and was swelling by the minute. That evening when Nas returned, neither of us said a word to the other. The next day Nas wanted to talk it out, and he suggested dinner.

"I don't know, Nas, doesn't Eric Smith have someplace to be?" I asked.

"Carm, what are you talking about? I told you I was in the projects *all night*. Come on, I'll take you to Jimmy's."

"Where am I going with an eye jammy? Look at my face."

"Carm, I'm so sorry. I didn't mean to hit you, I don't know what came over me. I just lost it. I swear on my daughter I'll never put my hands on you again."

I pulled myself together and we headed up to Jimmy's Bronx Café. Nas asked the host for his most quiet table and we were quickly seated. "Carm, I want to talk about you tonight."

"About me?"

We discussed what I liked and disliked, what I desired and what made me happy. He really tried to get inside my head. He insisted that he wanted us to be together, get married, have more children and that he was going to change his ways. I loved Nas and he was making an effort. Why give up now? I had always dreamt of having a family, so why not give it one more try?

· · ·

A few weeks later Capitol Records announced the termination of its urban music department and let thirty employees go, including me. I was actually relieved, I was tired of working full time. The layoff freed me up to spend time with Destiny.

Nas had a new group, The Firm, masterminded by Steve

Stoute, who nimbly finagled himself into the role of Nas's manager. Steve, whom Nas described simply as corny, was certainly no street thug, but he wasn't corny. He was focused and was actually a handsome man. Steve had an odd nervous tic and would tap his foot continuously. Steve and Tone, one of Track Master's producers, had created The Firm, which featured Foxy Brown and AZ. I'd had known AZ since back when he worked as a teleoperator, of course, but I had never met Foxy. Nas introduced me to her at the studio one evening. She was a cute brown-skinned girl with the prettiest eyes I'd ever seen. When I heard her rhyme, I said, "Wow! She is no joke."

Nas wasn't so impressed. "You can take a girl like Foxy, put her in a bowl, add a few ingredients, mix it up, and come up with another hitmaker." Who did Nas think he was fooling? Foxy was a talented MC and Nas was just insecure. He wouldn't have been working with her if that weren't the case.

By July we had moved and were settled in our new spot, *It Was Written* had dropped and once again Nas was back to his old tricks, rarely coming home, ignoring Destiny and me. We were a hobby of his, not a responsibility. His fleeting appearances in Destiny's life earned him the nickname "Uncle Daddy" among my family members. I objected at first, but eventually had to admit that Nas simply lacked parental instinct. One night Destiny had a bronchial and sinus infection that congested her so badly I took her to the emergency room. We got back to the house at five A.M. and found that Nas had just dragged himself home.

"Oh good, you're home," I said. "I need to go over to fill a prescription at the twenty-four-hour pharmacy. Just try to soothe Destiny till I'm back."

"Carm, just take her with you." The remote gaze that once indicated greatness to me now conveyed only coldness.

The road beckoned with the release of Nas's second LP and as usual, he bragged about how he was going to take Destiny and me on the road with him. When he went off alone on tour, I wasn't surprised but couldn't help feeling devastated.

Moving back to Long Island had its pros and cons. Although Queens was cool, it was definitely too local. Everyone knew where we lived, and their unannounced visits became a total nuisance. Still, I missed the company of my girlfriends.

Most days I reclined indoors, wallowing in endless self-pity. I was a mess and couldn't quite put my finger on the root of the problem. Maybe a small portion of my reclusive behavior had to do with my new dependence on Nas, after all, he was now the breadwinner. Don't get me wrong, I was relieved that I no longer had to rise every morning at the break of dawn and trudge to work every day after getting a few hours of restless sleep. When Mrs. Jones moved in, Nas had resorted to sleeping on the couch while Destiny and his mother shared our room. I didn't miss those days, that's for sure.

To get out of the house I took Destiny to see Mrs. Jones. Jabari's girlfriend, Shelly, was living at their place and had become like a sister to me. Shelly was very small and soft with slanted eyes and a cute button nose. Her warm smile alone could put me at ease. The trouble was I'd already internalized Nas's behavior. I'd come to believe I could never leave Nas, yet I hated myself for my dependence on someone so unworthy of it.

I decided I needed to talk to someone and called Risa. Ironically, she told me she'd just been released from the hospital after attempting suicide. Like me, she felt lonely and was in desperate need of attention.

Later that night, I thought deeply about my conversation with Risa. I wasn't happy and still couldn't identify the real problem. The next day I convinced myself I'd hit rock bottom. I went to the medicine cabinet and grabbed a bottle of sleeping pills.

One way that you can gauge the seriousness of a suicide attempt is by how long it takes the person to call a friend. My attempt was clearly a half-hearted one, because within a few minutes I was on the line with Rennette. My news created the intended scare: Rennette went ballistic and called an ambulance. Before long I was in a hospital bed with my hands strapped to its sides. A nurse pried my mouth open and a doctor inserted a long tube down my throat. It was the worst feeling in the world. I had no idea that this would be the end result of my cry for attention.

As I lay there having my stomach pumped inside out, I thought, *Bitch, this is what you get. Now you are the center of attention, are you satisfied?* By this time, my whole family had arrived and were waiting nervously in the lounge. When Sha Sha and my grandmother entered my room, I was too ashamed to face them so I closed my eyes and pretended to sleep.

"Carmen, I know you hear me," Sha Sha said in the same

tone of voice she might have used when I was five. "Ma, she ain't 'sleep."

Papa Lenny visited next. I had no trouble facing him, probably because there was no disgrace he hadn't already experienced firsthand.

"You're no different than anyone," he said. "We all feel helpless sometimes."

His words were a balm. But that night I was alone again in the hospital with time for some hard thinking. Destiny. What had I done? They could take Destiny away from me. I had to admit, I had gone way too far. I was ashamed of what I had done and didn't want to talk about it to anyone.

Then with stunning clarity the truth hit me: My disease was in assuming Nas was my only cure. I couldn't wait to get out of the hospital and start living again.

Before I could leave, I had to convince the hospital psychiatrist that I was in fact sane. The next morning we quickly came to the consensus that I was suffering from a chronic case of postpartum depression. By the time the psychiatrist signed my release papers, Nas had arrived and took me home. The ride home was quite awkward.

"Why did you do that, Carm?" Nas asked repeatedly. "Is it my fault? Am I doing something wrong?"

I'd been desperate for more understanding from Nas. Now that he was right beside me, I didn't know how to articulate my frustration, resentment, dependency, love. How could I describe the tangled feelings that led me to such a hopeless act? There was no quick and easy explanation.

"Here, this is for you." Nas put a gold gift box with a red ribbon on my lap.

I opened it. A platinum tennis bracelet with oval diamonds.

"Nas, it's gorgeous," I said.

But I didn't say anything else. I was emotionally drained and what I really desired was his time. No amount of verbal communication would have conveyed that. He needed to come to this conclusion on his own. I couldn't force Nas to spend time with us and all the gifts in the world wouldn't have made a difference.

Destiny spent the night with Mrs. Jones and Nas went back out on the road. Once again I was home alone, but this time I felt much different. I had gained a new passion for life as well as motherhood. The experience had put a new spin on things and lifted a heavy burden—one that I had carried for so long and from which I was glad to be free.

I received an especially concerned call from Steve Stoute. Like Nas, he wanted to know why I'd tried to take my life. Steve and I were real cool at that time, so I confided in him. It felt so good to unload. Socializing, I realized, was the only antidote to isolation.

The final call was from Rennette, who wondered if I felt up to going to Tracey's birthday party later that night. I grabbed my purse and went to the spa for a quick tan, manicure and pedicure. I got my outfit together and was at the club by midnight. All of Tracey's associates and close friends were in the club, including Puff, Rhonda and Steve. I even spotted Left Eye from TLC. When Steve saw me, he did a double take.

Here I was getting my party on only a few hours out of the hospital. I just smiled in his direction and hit the dance floor. No more apologies for meeting my own needs. Simply enjoying myself was a form of therapy, the cure to some of my woes.

CHAPTER 10

Back To Eden

. . . .

NAS AND I FLIPPED the coin of love and hate all the time. But the love shared between us never changed. When the phone rang the day after the party I just knew it was him. Surely Steve would report back to Nas and tell him that I was a guest at Tracey's shindig. Steve and I were good friends, but he was Nas's friend first and foremost. I was ready for the questions.

Instead it was my friend Danae, calling to fill me in on her recent trip to Virginia. We spoke of friends I had met on a previous visit there. Marlon, Arnie, and Lamont were all cool as hell. The final member of the cipher, Bubba Chuck, was locked up during my visit but was always on the phone with Marlon or Lamont. "Damn, this nigga must have his section on lock," I'd said to Danae. They were on the phone for what seemed like forever.

As Danae went on about her recent trip, she mentioned that Bubba Chuck was home from jail and wanted to meet me.

"Me? He's never even seen me, Danae." *Not another blind date,* I thought.

"Well, I happened to have a couple pics with me down there." Danae was notorious for carrying around photos, props for her self-appointed role as Cupid to all her friends. "He really, really wants to meet you."

"What does he look like, Danae?"

"Carm, trust me, you won't be disappointed. He's a dime."

Danae had a way with words. I didn't trust her. He could very well be some big, tall, doofy basketball player that will squash little ole' me.

She went on to say that he had played ball since his youth, would soon be playing for the 76ers and had just signed an endorsement deal with Reebok. Now I was even more wary. Sports were not an interest of mine so it all sounded foreign to me. Plus, I already had a man.

"Chuck will be up in New York to do some press in three days. It won't hurt to meet him, Carm."

Over the next couple of days, I surfed through the sports channels trying to find the mysterious Bubba Chuck, but came up with nothing. Newspapers didn't turn up any stories, either. The lack of information on Chuck only intensified my deep-seated mistrust of blind dates.

Back when I was in high school, my cousin Felicia set me up on a blind date with her boyfriend's friend Devine. Before the date, I found out Devine hustled and had a few hand-to-hand workers on his block, but so did a lot of guys in the neighborhood. Like most of us, Devine didn't have a car, so he picked me up in a gypsy cab. Gypsy cabdrivers were like those butler characters in old movies: no matter what happened, they'd keep a straight face and go right on driving. In the cab on the way to the city, Devine told me what he had planned for the night: a Central Park horse-drawn carriage ride followed by dinner at a place in Little Italy. It was a dream date.

We got out of the cab on the southern edge of the park. Devine gave me his arm to step up into a quaint red carriage with yellow wheels. A bouquet of fresh flowers perched on the edge of the driver's seat. We clip-clopped through the park under a night sky that even had a few stars visible, the few bright enough to outshine the city's lights.

"It's like another period in time," I said. "I'm half-thinking we're going to come out of the park to gaslights and ladies in bonnets."

"And Sherlock Holmes or some shit like that!" Devine added. He reached over to take my hand. When he did, a gun fell out of his pants, hitting the carriage floor and firing off into the dark wall of trees beside the road. The horse bucked wildly, causing the carriage to swerve and bounce out of control. The driver struggled at the reins until he finally calmed the animal.

As soon as we'd stopped, Devine bolted. "Carm, let's go!" Devine grabbed my hand to pull me off the carriage. We ran as fast as we could back to the gypsy cab that was waiting for us a few blocks away. It seemed best to get out of the city, so we headed back to Queens.

"I feel sorry for that carriage guy," I said.

"He got paid in advance," Devine answered, as if that compensated for all the trouble.

Me and Tyson Beckford at a BAMN Clothing Photo Shoot (NYC).

. . . .

Nas and me at the China Grill (NYC) celebrating his birthday.

Me and Destiny at Disney World, Florida.

Destiny enjoying a nap—first class.

· · · · · · · · · ·

Nas and Destiny at the beach.

Nas and Destiny at Universal Studios, LA.

Me, Nas, Destiny, my cousin Andrea, and friend Ebony at Disney World, Florida.

· · · · · · · · · ·

Destiny's birthday party at school (me, Nas, Destiny, and friend Megan Good).

Me and Tarja about to hit the town in LA.

Nas and me on 125th Street.

. . . .

Me, Tarja, Ruby, and Danae back at Justin's.

Nas at home, chilling.

· · · · · · · · · ·

Nas and I on our first vacation in the Bahamas.

Nas, Destiny, and me.

Me and Nas at Benihana.

· · · · · · · · ·

Nas and his mom at my family's barbeque.

Destiny's Halloween party: Destiny, me, and my goddaughter Ashley.

Me, Tarja, and Rennette back on 125th Street.

Me, Danae, Ruby, and Shelly at my favorite restaurant, Justin's (NYC). Picture taken by Shawn Carter.

Destiny's birthday party at Fun Zone: Nas, Destiny, and me.

Me and Dina on tour in Sicily.

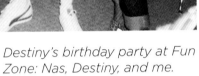

Nas and me at Mariah Carey's New Year's Eve party.

Back home, Devine asked if I still wanted to get something to eat. *Fuck it,* I thought, *what else could happen on this crazy night?* We headed to the Buccaneer Diner on Astoria Boulevard.

On the way, Devine called up to the driver. "Hey man, can you slow down?"

"What's going on?" I asked.

"Nothing," Devine said to me. To the driver he said, "Just go around the block and drive slow past that corner store." The driver nodded and complied—he and Devine clearly had some kind of history. When we neared the store, Devine reached into his pants and pulled out his gun. The crowd in front of the store didn't know what was hitting them as Devine fired shot after shot from our passing cab.

"Are you fucking crazy?" I screamed, as everyone on the boulevard ran for cover. That early experience was enough to put me off blind dates forever.

I called Danae. "I can't find anything in the news about this Bubba Chuck. The blind date is off!"

Danae laughed. "Fool, his real name is Allen Iverson."

Back to my research. When his given name didn't turn up any information either, I was ready to give up and planned to flake out on the meeting that night. This blind date was just too blind. So when the time came for our mini meet and greet I would be a *no show!* Danae would be pissed—oh well.

Danae must have anticipated my evasive maneuver. When she called to make plans for the night, Allen was on the line with her. So much for my plan! We talked for about fifteen minutes, and the conversation seemed intriguing enough but the actual subject matter was irrelevant. I went soft just at the sound of his voice. He had a southern drawl, its soothing charm roughened around the edges by a slightly abrasive thuggishness. Sexy. I felt desired for the first time in a long time.

That night Danae, Rennette and I headed to Manhattan to meet the mysterious Bubba Chuck. On the ride up in the hotel elevator we all gave ourselves a quick look in the panel mirrors. As usual, our hair had stayed in place and our butts had retained their roundness since we'd last checked thirty minutes ago. I wore tight blue jeans, a fitted, sleeveless, cropped peach T-shirt, a pair of Gucci stilettos and matching bag. A fresh coat of lip gloss and I was good to go.

We were all giggling and laughing like schoolgirls as we made our way to his room. Rennette even started poplocking, dancing down the hallway. We knocked on his door and finally Allen Iverson stood in the doorway before us.

Danae had been right, but she had understated it. He was hot, red-hot! He was wearing a crisp white Reebok T-shirt—apparently his endorsement deal was a 24/7 job—and a platinum chain with a diamond-packed medallion. His matching bracelet and pinky ring were just as icy. Allen had the raw goods, too: a perfect body and a face that would still be cute when he was eighty. I might have stood there transfixed forever if Danae hadn't barged in past him and quickly introduced everyone.

We all sat in the suite and made small talk for about five minutes. I was a little nervous and went to the bathroom to pull it together. Without warning, Allen busted into the bathroom, walked to the toilet, pulled down his pants and took a piss.

"Ummm . . . excuuuse me," I haughtily asked.

His only reply was a simple "What??" like he didn't notice

he was relieving himself in front of a complete stranger. Was he that comfortable around me already? As shocked as I was, I was even more curious and took a discreet peek to see what he was working with. My findings were more than satisfactory. I quickly dried my hands and made it out of the bathroom before Allen was finished.

When I came out, Danae blurted, "Yo, he is feeling you, Carm. He was like, 'Good lookin', Danae, she's a dime.' " Rennette was at the mirror combing her hair. She shook her head. "Carm, that nigga look good as hell."

"Don't be looking at my man, bitch," I said, laughing.

We headed out for dinner in Allen's chauffeur-driven white limo. Allen talked without pause, pointing out anything that caught his eye on the sidewalk. Then his words began to take on rhythm. So that was his true aspiration! Being the #1 pick in the NBA draft wasn't enough. He wanted to be a rapper. All the way to the restaurant, Allen freestyled nonstop, mostly funny little rhymes about whatever trivial thing was happening out on the street. It was becoming clear that Allen always made sure he was the star of the show. But for all Allen's arrogance, his fun-loving, scrappy character made him irresistible.

Allen's Reebok rep, T, met us at Coldwater's, a seafood place, and whisked us back to a secluded area so quickly that only a couple of diners spotted Allen. The bustling restaurant had hardwood floors, maritime-themed prints on the walls and was known for good lobster. Its white-paper–covered tables weren't designed for eating so much as feeding. But Allen and I were too busy flirting to eat much. The attraction was mutual and strong.

We went back to Allen's room for cocktails after dinner and

I soon told him it was time to go, I had to get home to Destiny. But Allen, on the other hand, didn't seem to have any reservations about jumping into bed on the first night. I declined but he only let me leave after making me promise to return the next day. He handed over his room key to formalize the welcome. Even though I was in a rush to get Destiny, I was in no rush to leave Allen. I was on cloud nine the entire ride home. I picked up Destiny, went home and relived the evening over and over again as I got ready for bed.

The next morning when I woke, I was still on my high, with a romantic montage of thoughts of Allen and Carm playing in my head. It was interrupted by a couple of quick scenes from my history with Nas, but they passed quickly and thoughts of Allen resumed. But there was no guilt. It was like Olu said, we were all free to do what we wanted, when we wanted. Nas had certainly taken a page out of Olu's book. Now Olu, Nas and I were all on the same page. I loved Nas but I loved myself more, and I was very, very much into Allen.

Later that day Danae and I headed back to Allen's hotel in Manhattan. I used the key that he had given me the previous night to enter his room. It was empty, but as soon as I took a seat on the bed, Allen and T burst into the room. "Caught y'all," he said, laughing.

He and T carried in a number of shopping bags filled with promotional items from Reebok. It was like Christmas. Allen was hosting a show at the Palladium nightclub later that night and invited us to come along.

"Carm, you and Danae want to roll with us?" Allen asked.

"Cool, but I have to go home and change," I insisted.

Allen reached into his pocket, pulled out a wad of cash and slapped it in my hand. "Just go get something to wear real quick and come right back."

Danae and I flagged down a cab and went straight to Saks. Without any financial limitations, the perfect clothes jumped right out at me: a lilac suede halter top, black suede boy-shorts and black suede knee-high boots. We changed at the hotel, then we all hopped in the limo and drove straight to the club. The entrance was packed, so we circled around the block hoping to find a secure back entry. It was just as packed in the back of the club as it was in the front. Allen, Marlon, Danae, Rennette and I stood beside the limo and waited for T to do his thing. That's when I noticed a mob of dudes across the street sizing up Marlon and Allen, whose gleaming jewelry looked like a payday under the streetlights. Ramel, a friend of mine, headed over from the clique.

"Carm, you here with that nigga Allen?" Ramel asked.

"Yeah, that's my friend. Why?"

"That's your business. But you see them niggas across the street right there? They about to set it on ya man Allen."

I sucked my teeth. "Why don't you just tell them to chill?"

"I can't stop them niggas from doing what they want to do."

I thanked Ramel for trying to look out and returned to Allen's side. There was no beating around the bush, I got straight to the point. "You see those dudes over there?" I asked.

"Yeah, I peeped them grilling us," Allen answered.

"They're from Brooklyn, the one I was just talking to is a

friend of mine, and he said them niggas are about to rob you and that we should leave before shit gets crazy."

"I ain't going fuckin' nowhere!" Allen bawled out. "Let them niggas come over here on some bullshit, if they wanna. I got somethin' for them niggas."

T interrupted him. "I think her friend is right. We need to leave. It's not worth it. I am not trying to get killed out here over no bullshit."

Allen was defiant. "Then get in the car, nigga, and you won't be in it. But I ain't going nowhere."

Allen meant every word. We stood rooted in that spot until long after the fire marshal arrived and shut down the party. The pack from Brooklyn broke out. We all got back in the limo, drinking and riding around the city for what seemed hours. I have to say, seeing Allen in rare form at the Palladium was such a turn-on. I couldn't wait to be alone with him. Finally, we dropped everyone off and headed back to the hotel.

By the time the door closed we were all over each other. Before I knew it, my top came off, followed by my shorts, then everything else.

Allen was lean and muscled, a warrior, with tattoos and battle scars. Just looking at him got me excited. His body was scrumptious. His kiss was intoxicating and I felt like I was melting. Our antics took us from one side of the bed to the other. I couldn't get enough of this man. He was so physically strong he thought nothing of picking me up and creating the most erotic of poses. When he finally possessed me I was so ready. He filled me completely and our rhythm was perfect. Allen was above average in size but his gift was girth and technique. His sliding and swerving thrusts hit me in spots I didn't know I had. And this was only round one.

In round two he picked me up and swiftly carried me over to a table, perching me on its edge. I was ready, I couldn't get enough of Allen. In his excitement he scooped me off the table with one hand, holding me up by my hips and lower back to straddle his standing frame. This man was off the hook!

Satisfied, we fell back on the bed. Looking into those amber eyes, I teased, "That was goooood."

"You think we're done? Oh, we ain't done!"

He buried his face in my neck in spontaneous affection, which got round three going. By now I needed a battery to keep up with the energetic Bubba Chuck. After that third round, I was so stoned with satisfaction that I was out like a light as soon as my head hit the pillow.

A few hours later there was a knock on the door. Allen leapt out of bed and opened it. T stood there frozen. Allen was butt naked and so was I.

"Allen, you-you're running late for your flight," T stuttered.

"Close the door!" I yelled, wondering how many naked girls T had already glimpsed during these wake-up visits. Allen quickly showered, dressed and was ready to head to the airport. He gave me a kiss and said he would call me once he got to Virginia. But when he got to the door, he hesitated, turning around.

"Can I get some more?"

I was flattered. "You sure can, get over here!"

"Nas ever tell you, you got some good stuff?" he asked.

"Not in words," I replied. After he left for the airport, I went back to sleep. An hour later the telephone rang, scaring the hell out of me. I didn't answer at first, but the caller was persistent. Maybe it was Danae. I picked up the phone.

"What are you doing answering my phone?" Allen hissed.

"Whatever, I thought you were Danae."

"I'm just kidding, stay where you at, I'm on my way back. I missed my flight fucking with you."

"See you when you get here," I said.

Allen arrived an hour later. He got back in the bed. He had a lot of stamina and couldn't seem to get enough of me. We cuddled, talked and went back to sleep. Hours later we woke up, ordered room service and had sex again and again and again.

Heading home that afternoon, I felt refreshed and lively, as though change was definitely in the air.

CHAPTER 11

Change of Heart

. . . .

AFTER MEETING ALLEN, SOMETHING changed. Actually everything changed. The new experience was just what I needed. In a nutshell, Allen was the bomb! He had a wonderful sense of humor, was very spontaneous and no matter who entered the room, Allen always maintained his true sense of being. He was real. Our time was sweet, but this too would eventually come to an end. When Allen left for basketball camp and Nas went back on the road, once again it was just me and Destiny.

It was a hot and sticky August night. Danae, Tarja, Risa and I were on our way to a Def Jam artist showcase at the Roxy. We were making a pit stop to pick up Rennette at Santa Fe, a Mexican restaurant on Queens Boulevard where she'd recently started working.

"Who's gonna be there?" Danae asked, rolling the car window down.

"Who cares as long as the music's good," I answered.

I was just happy to be out with my girls. Meeting Allen had inspired my own private renaissance. I'd registered for fall classes at Fashion Institute of Technology in Manhattan. I had renewed energy and enthusiasm for everything, including hanging with my friends. I was learning that a social life and motherhood weren't necessarily mutually exclusive. Sha Sha was an excellent mother; she managed her social life, a career and raised us singlehandedly. The key was balancing responsible parenting with self-fulfillment. An overly nurturing but personally frustrated mother figure wouldn't do Destiny much good anyway.

When we pulled up to the restaurant, Rennette met us at the entrance with some bad news. "Sorry, I gotta work overtime," she said. "Can't go tonight." Rennette seemed a little off and was clearly upset about something besides missing the showcase.

"What's the matter, Rennette?" I asked.

"I am fucking pissed, that's what. Do you know that Mike is in here with Angie Martinez from Hot 97?"

"Mike Geronimo?" I asked. "Like on a date?"

"Yes." Rennette had every reason to be upset. Mike was a childhood friend of mine who had recently fathered a child with Rennette's best friend, Barbara. Mike acknowledged the child but was otherwise a complete deadbeat. Angie was a radio DJ who aired everyone else's sins, yet she was herself hooking up with a deadbeat baby-father.

"I'm ready to fuck him and Angie both up," Rennette threatened. Avoiding an altercation with Rennette was like dodging a bullet.

By this time Mike and Angie were leaving the restaurant and ran into us at the entrance. Mike greeted me with his usual warmth. "Wassup, Carm? What's going on?"

"I'm good, what's up with you?" I returned his hug while keeping an eye on Rennette, who was struggling to maintain her composure. Angie politely excused herself, telling Mike she was going to get the car.

Rennette erupted. "Mike, how you got time to be out with the next bitch, but you ain't got time to check for your son?"

Her rant rolled right off Mike, who was as laid-back and easy-going as ever—though he did make a quick exit when Angie showed up.

"Aight, Carm," Mike said. "I'm out. Tell ya brother to call me."

Mike left, but was back in a just a minute or two saying Angie's car had run out of gas. He asked if I would give him a ride to the gas station while Angie waited. Before taking him, I asked Risa to keep watch on Rennette.

On the ride to the gas station I asked, "So what's up with you and homegirl?"

Mike cracked a smile out the side of his mouth. "Carm, you know how it goes down." He thought I was complimenting him on his hookup with Angie!

"Not Angie, fool," I said. "Barbara. When are you going to go see your son?"

There was no response. There usually wasn't. The girlfriend code required that Rennette and I give him hell about his fatherly duties. Just a few weeks later Tarja and I would be out in

Shelter Island helping Rennette storm her boyfriend Erick on a love holiday with another girl.

Erick and Rennette had been dating for a few months. She was in love. When we pulled into the driveway we spotted Erick through the glass double doors. And he wasn't alone. Rennette was on fire. Before I could fully put the car in park, Rennette was at the front door pounding the hell out of it with her fists. The couple refused to open the door. Frustrated and heartbroken, Rennette reached down, grabbed the biggest rock she could find and smashed the front door glass. She stuck her hand through the shattered screen and unlocked the door. That's when all hell broke loose. By the time Tarja and I entered the house Rennette was in the living room with Erick and the mysterious woman. Without warning, Rennette reached back and punched the girl in the face, she then turned to Erick and slapped the holy fire out of him. It was on. Tarja and I were all over the chick, while Rennette pounced on Erick, who was flat on his back trying to defend himself from Rennette's blows. The mystery woman somehow got loose from Tarja and I and made a dash for the telephone. That's when Tarja pulled out her switchblade and cut the phone wire. That put an end to that. Rennette finally let up on Erick and there was a moment of peace.

"Erick, pack ya shit, we dropping this bitch off, and me and you are going to finish this later!"

They packed and Rennette and Erick dropped the girl off at the ferry. I, on the other hand, felt rather ridiculous. Not to mention the poor girl had a speed knot the size of a golf ball. I found out later that the girl had been warned once before by Rennette. Still, it didn't excuse our immature behavior.

We headed on to the Roxy in Manhattan. We all loved the club. I spotted an old friend, Ty Ty, whom I'd met back in high school through Danae. After we were nestled in a cozy corner, a stranger marched right up and invaded our intimate circle. He stood with his arms folded, chewing on a toothpick with a mouth that was large by any measure.

We were all like, "Hello?" *Who is this fool?* I thought.

Ty Ty spoke up. "Oh, this is my man Jay-Z." We all said hello and then ignored him, keeping the talk moving within our group. As we were walking to the bar, I noticed Jay-Z right behind me, practically on my heels. Was this guy going to follow me all night long? My sneering facial expression should have indicated a lack of interest. Jay-Z attempted to strike up a conversation.

My reaction was off the shoulder. "I have a boyfriend," I said bluntly.

"So?" he replied. I walked away from him at least five times. I even hid behind pillars, but he would just stick his head around from the other side, grinning big.

He was extremely persistent. I finally broke down and gave him the two minutes he craved and listened to his pitch. I figured the night would be over soon and I'd never have to see this character again.

"I'm out of breath chasing you around this place."

I just laughed at his humor. This boy was persistant. By the time he took a breath, I had learned that his name was Shawn

Carter, he was from Brooklyn, born and raised, could ride a bike since he was five years old, he owned his own record company, didn't write his rhymes down, never been in love, was retiring after his second album and lived with his cousin.

Shawn's two minutes turned into five, then fifteen as we talked and joked easily. For me, what stood out the most was his tone of voice, which I loved. Then it was showtime, which pretty much let me off the hook. Shawn's performance was cool. He was a little stiff, but all in all it was a good show.

The crowd began to disperse after the performance. Near the exit I saw Shawn talking to Bridgette, a friend I'd met through Shelly.

"There you are, Carm," Bridgette said. "Girl, I've been looking all over for you. This is my friend Jay-Z."

"We already met," I replied.

"So what's up, can I get ya number?" Shawn would not quit.

"I have a boyfriend," I said sternly.

"We covered that," he said with a laugh. Shawn asked Bridgette for a pen, scribbled his number on a piece of paper, and handed both back to her.

"Make sure your friend calls me," he mumbled as he walked off.

Bridgette handed me the number. "Listen, I know Shawn, and he's mad cool. Brooklyn niggas are cheap, don't get me wrong, but just call him, Carm, and see what happens. He knows that you already have a man, but practically begged me to hook this up. So please just call him."

"I don't think so," I repeated. No matter how much Bridgette pleaded, I was not interested and was not budging and that was that.

• • •

The next morning I made plans to have breakfast at Rennette's. Destiny, who was two at the time, had asked if she could spend the day with Grandma Ann, which is what she called Mrs. Jones, so I dropped her off there on my way to Rennette's. Before leaving I scrambled around the house for my house keys and came across the folded piece of paper with Shawn's number on it. "I think I'll hold on to this." I slipped the number back in my purse and was out the door. En route, Nas called on my cell phone.

"You are playing yaself," Nas barked. "Where were you last night? And don't lie because I called and your sister answered the phone. You was out shaking ya ass all night when you should have been home with Destiny." Blah blah blah, I had tuned Nas out. There was no reasoning with him. His idea of the ideal woman was pregnant, barefoot and in the kitchen. "No man wants a chick with kids, Carm, don't you know that." His double standard was unchanging: Men were hounds according to birthright but women should remain angels regardless.

After hanging up on Nas, I pulled my little piece of paper out of my purse with Shawn's number on it and stuffed it in my back pocket. I'd be giving him a call later.

After I hugged Destiny goodbye, I talked to Shelly for a minute. Mrs. Jones came wearily into the living room. Her face lacked its usual glow.

"What's wrong, Mrs. Jones?" I asked.

"I'm okay. Just tired. I sure wish Nas would retire me. What he wears on his arm, I have to work a whole year to earn." Mrs. Jones was getting up in age and her full-time job at the post office was starting to wear on her. "I just can't wait until I can retire and get my house and start my garden."

Jabari stormed in from the bedroom. "Ma, Nas is never going to buy you a house," he said bitterly. "I don't know why you keep saying that. He's never going to buy you your own crib. He'll move you into his spot, but that's about it."

Mrs. Jones was hurt. She kept a stiff upper lip, but her eyes began to tear.

"Jabari, why would you say that?" Shelly demanded.

"It's true!" Jabari felt he was speaking truth to power and wouldn't be stopped. "And I'm telling you right now, Carm, if something happens with you and my brother and ya'll break up, he ain't gonna wanna see you do good either. Even though you have his daughter, if you ain't with my brother, he's not gonna want to see ya'll chilling in a house or chilling, period."

Mrs. Jones started to sob and Jabari finally realized he had said too much.

"I'm sorry, Ma," he consoled. "I take that back. Nas is going to buy you a crib. Okay, Ma?"

At first I thought Jabari was hating on Nas out of pure jealousy. Then it hit me. For years Jabari had been instrumental to Nas's career but had never been rewarded for his time and effort. Jabari was Nas's one-man A&R team. In the studio, he not only screened the music but conceived songs, wrote hooks and choruses and in some cases contributed actual verses. Nas had repaid Jabari for his services by buying him a used car and giving him an allowance of a few hundred dollars a week. Jabari wasn't concerned with getting the proper credit on Nas's albums, but he did want to be compensated fairly. If Nas would hit him off, Jabari could do what he wanted to do, which was to pursue his own career.

Once things settled at the Jones's I left for Rennette's place. On the drive I recounted Jabari's words over and over again. Although I knew Nas very well, his brother knew him even better. I had to remind myself that Nas was human and very capable of being the person that Jabari depicted. Being famous did not make him immune to being human. I then tried to put myself in his shoes. Everything that glitters isn't gold. Nas was also under pressure from the strains of everyday life, from friends, fans and his record company. He lived what most called the fabulous life, but Nas had to work in order to maintain his lifestyle. He had to find producers, come up with hits, and leave town at the drop of a dime in order to provide for his family. Under the wrong circumstances, if he were pulled in too many directions, Nas probably was capable of becoming the grudging person Jabari suggested, even toward his daughter.

When I got to Rennette's apartment, she asked me about the Def Jam party and I mentioned my conversation with Shawn.

"Do you have his number?" Rennette asked. I pulled it from my pocket. "Page him now," she ordered.

I did. Shawn called right back. "Hey, Shawn, it's me, Carm."

"Hold on, I'm on the other line with my lawyer." He was back with me in three seconds. "What's up, Carm? I didn't think I was going to hear from you."

After speaking briefly, we realized he lived in the same building as Rennette's boyfriend Erick and made plans to meet there later that evening. But that night, when I pulled up to their three-story brick building on State Street, I had a fit of paranoia. What if someone saw me and told Nas? I parked several blocks away, called Shawn and asked him to meet me at Erick's apartment.

Shawn calmed me down and we headed to a little Greek spot in the Village. Its dimmed lights, draped silk panels and midriff-baring waitresses gave it a sensual and exotic atmosphere. The aroma of the food was delicious. As the waitresses floated back and forth with plates of food, my appetite increased. Unfortunately, nothing was recognizable, and I wasn't taking any chances on an allergic reaction.

"I'm not really hungry," I said to Shawn.

"Really? Well, you seem to be enjoying your wine."

I drank the night away while we talked. Nas and I always discussed Nas. With Shawn, I wanted to quickly establish a precedent of talking about me. So when he brought up his career, I flipped it.

"I worked in the industry," I said. "I used to model."

"And you're a mother," he noted. "That's a full-time job in itself." This Shawn character appeared to be wise beyond his years. Shawn was very warm and extremely humble, with a wonderful sense of humor. Over dinner I decided he and I would be good friends for a very long time. We went back to Erick's house talking and laughing. I was in no condition to drive home, so I decided to spend the night at Erick's. Shawn and I sat on the couch and pretended to watch television. Before long I drifted off to sleep. I woke up with Shawn kissing me. His lips were so soft and luscious and I began to melt into him. He hands began to roam but I wasn't ready and put an end to that quick. "Its getting late, Shawn. I'm about to crash here on Erick's couch. I'll give you a call tomorrow."

"You can sleep on my couch," he whispered.

"Pretty sure," I replied and gave him a look that said, "I don't think so!"

After he left I changed into one of Erick's extra-large T-shirts and passed out on the couch.

I spent more time with Shawn over the next couple of weeks. The more I got to know about him, the more I liked—but he was definitely staying in the "friend zone." Unfortunately, the more time I spent with him the sexier he seemed to me. Shawn had the allure of a grand stature, of a man with a plan. He knew what he wanted from life and was confident and driven. Nothing is sexier on a man than a strong sense of purpose.

It turned out Shawn and Nas shared a taste in more than women. They each had a Lexus GS 300: Shawn's was silver and Nas's gold.

As far as I was concerned. Shawn was just another struggling MC trying to work his way up to stardom. He could have put on a million fronts, which he did from time to time, but still I'd see right through him.

He often bragged about his many women and claimed he

had a girlfriend. But she never called when we were together and there were no combs or signs of her in his crib. One day he claimed he'd broken up with her. He was new to the business, he said, and knew it would put a strain on the relationship. The subtext of these discussions was always the same. Shawn: I'm trying to get a reaction out of you. Carmen: We're just friends. You're not my man, so I don't care. The information he provided clearly told me that he was insecure.

His view of women was also very one-sided. We would get into these huge debates and arguments. We'd even stop speaking every so often, then most times when he called to make up, I had forgotten we were even beefing.

What I hated was turning down his invitations. Shawn would invite me to places I dreamed of visiting and I would always decline for fear of our little secret being exposed. It was a frustrating feeling, considering Nas never took me and Destiny anywhere.

What made Shawn so unique from the other men I had dated was that he became my best friend. He really listened to me and when I spoke he would look intently into my eyes. It was almost like he was recording my every word to memory. I had never been with a man who was so attuned to my thoughts and feelings. It worked both ways; I really cared about Shawn and respected and valued his opinions. It felt like I was in my first adult relationship. When I met Nas we were damn near still teenagers and that set the tone for our lives.

Although I still loved Nas, I was no longer in love. I had always hoped that we would be the family that we both dreamed of but realized Destiny was the glue holding us together. I knew what it was like to grow up fatherless and wished to spare her the experience. The reality was Nas and I were together but living separate lives and that made room for Shawn.

Although the summer was near its end, it was just the beginning for Shawn and me. When Shawn called and invited me to his cookout, I was delighted to hear from him and accepted the invitation. I had put Shawn on hold for too long, and seeing him always tickled my spirit. I ended up inviting a few of the girls. Rennette was practically living with Erick at the time, so neither one of them needed a formal invite. In order to avoid suspicion, I told my friends that Erick was having the barbeque. After all, Erick lived right across the courtyard. When we arrived the barbeque was well under way. Shawn was being a good host, Ty Ty was on grill duty, and the small crowd seemed to be enjoying themselves. It wasn't long before Erick joined us in the courtyard. He said hello and shook his head. I'm sure he was having Shelter Island flashbacks.

"Erick, you're not going to say hello to Tarja?" I asked.

"Oh, sorry, I didn't recognize her without her scarf and switchblade," he answered.

Tarja and I both laughed, then made our way through the party. Shawn and I exchanged glances every chance we got. Shortly after our arrival, he came over to make sure everyone was having a good time. How unexpectedly sweet he had turned out to be. We didn't hug or greet each other like we would normally do, though. No one knew about us and I wanted to keep it that way.

All throughout the evening, Shawn kept hinting for me to go up to his apartment. I shook my head no! every time. It just wasn't safe. This went on for a good while, until he finally came over to me and whispered, "Meet me upstairs. I'll go first."

I laughed. "Are you crazy? What if someone sees us?" However, two minutes later, I did what came naturally, slipped away and found myself in Shawn's bedroom. Shawn was already planted on the bed. I closed the door behind me and sat beside him. After a few minutes of kissing and groping, the door busted wide open. It was some chick I recognized from a video. She marched right into the room, grabbed a set of keys from the window ledge and stood before us. She looked pretty pissed. She was ice-grilling so hard, her face looked like stone. Shawn and I both looked at each other and my face read, "Nigga, if you make one move, I am so deadin' you." He sat there stunned with his mouth open. When Shawn continued to sit there mute she eventually gave up and left. But now I was pissed, not because he was with another chick but because I had a man and now my privacy was at risk. Without another word being spoken I went back to the barbeque.

"Where have you been?" Danae asked. "I've been looking all over for you."

"I was in the bathroom," I replied.

"I just came from the bathroom," she pried.

"Then I don't know how you missed me."

Danae was good for being observant. It was time to go!

But I hadn't seen the last of Shawn that night. He called on my way home from the barbeque and basically begged me to come back to Brooklyn. After many excuses and explanations in regard to the incident in his bedroom with the video chick, none of which I cared to hear, he finally convinced me to hang with him for the rest of the evening. But on my way back to Brooklyn, I caught a flat tire and ended up pulling off the highway and onto a street directly under the Brooklyn Bridge.

Okay, Carm, where the fuck are you? I panicked. It was pretty dark and there wasn't a soul in sight. I frantically called Shawn to come and fetch me.

"You are where, Carm?" he deadpanned.

"I don't know, Shawn, I live in Long Island. I'm under some bridge!"

"What bridge?"

"I don't know, I just got off the highway when I realized I had a flat."

"Alright, alright, I think I know where you are, it can be only one bridge. Just lock the doors, I'm on my way."

The next thing I knew Shawn was pulling up in a white van with his friends. They fixed my tire and Shawn and I drove my car back to Brooklyn.

Apparently I wasn't done being scolded. "You are crazy, you can't be pulling off the highway when you have a flat. When we get to the crib you're getting a beatin'."

All I could say was, "I can't wait." Nothing is sexier than a knight in shining armor coming to your rescue.

• • •

In September, Allen called with an invitation for Danae and me to meet him and Marlon at basketball camp in New Jersey, not too far from Atlantic City. I couldn't wait to see him again—I was like a fiend needing another hit of Bubba Chuck! Nas was coming home from tour and things between us were tense, thanks to Wendy Williams, a DJ on Hot 97 radio. Wendy Williams had announced on the air that Allen and a certain Queensbridge rapper's wife were shacking up while the rapper was hard at work on the road promoting his new album. Nas's colleague Foxy Brown had played the grim reaper of gossip, calling Nas immediately after she heard the radio report, even adding she'd seen a photo of Destiny and Allen together at a mall in Philly. She was attempting to give Nas information and play him at the same time.

Nas was furious when he called me. For the first time— it wouldn't be the last—I was forced to resort to the two-part method employed by cheating men everywhere: "Deny, deny, deny."

"Nas, Foxy is just a jealous bitch. Why are you listening to rumors anyway? Why are you questioning me unless you are out there doing something that you shouldn't be doing! Don't ask me questions out of your own sense of guilt."

He proceeded to curse me out as if I were a complete stranger, calling me a whore, slut, liar and so on.

"First of all you're never home and you never take us anywhere," I said. 'You're always in the streets hanging out with your stupid-ass friends. Maybe if you spent some quality time with your family, there would be no room for suspicion on my part or yours! We're not married, I don't see no ring on this finger. According to your father, we're not obligated." I knew Nas was out there, I've always known he was a cheater, so I had to let him fucking have it! I felt like, "What-eva, nigga. You do you and I'll do me."

There was no question after that blow up I was going to Atlantic City. But I was cutting it pretty close. Nas was due home Sunday night. If I left Thursday night, I'd have to be back early Sunday to beat him home. If not, I'd be back in the frying pan. The only other thing on my agenda besides Allen was giving this bitch Foxy a call. Oh, I would be calling her for sure!

CHAPTER 12

Acts of Faith

. . . .

ON THURSDAY DANAE AND I headed to Atlantic City to meet Allen and Marlon. In my eagerness I floored it the whole way. We arrived around midnight, valet parked and entered the hotel lobby, which was filled with 76ers ball players. They were everywhere. Seven-foot-tall men surrounded us, and I felt dwarfed by these beautiful giants.

"Wow, this is basketball camp," I said to Danae.

"All I want to know is when are we hitting the casino?"

A few of the players tried to holler at us and Danae played the bait, swishing her hips, adding a fresh coat of lip gloss. Danae loved being the center of attention.

"These niggas look good up in here," Danae went on.

"They're alright," I replied.

I put everyone on mute. My focus was on you know who!

We picked up the key Allen had left for us and made our way up to his suite. The room was empty, so Danae and I decided to do a little snooping around. We rummaged through the wastebaskets for condom wrappers or phone numbers, and searched for strands of hair on the pillows, lipstick on towels, and extra toothbrushes in the bathroom. In the midst of our search, the door opened. It was Allen. I quickly played off my snooping and pretended as if I were looking for a place to store my bags.

"When did ya'll get here?" Allen asked.

"Just a minute ago," I lied. He grabbed me, gave me a big hug and kiss. That alone made the whole drive worth it. Things only got better. For the rest of the evening, the four of us sipped on Cristal, ordered room service and enjoyed each other's company. The evening was starting to mellow when out of nowhere Danae came out with:

"So Chuck, what's up with you and this Foxy bitch, huh?" she asked.

If there had been an LP playing it would have screeched to a halt. Everything just stopped! I couldn't believe Danae. She was famous for blowing up the spot.

Foxy was definitely number one on my shit list, but this was not the time or place to discuss the Foxy beef. Besides, just the mention of her name blew my high.

"Nothing, I met her one time," Allen responded.

I watched Allen's body language closely as Danae went on. "Well, I heard her on the radio and she said that you and her were an item, and that you bought her a diamond ring and a necklace."

Allen jumped out of his seat. "Get the fuck outta here! I don't even know that girl."

"Well, she drops your name like she knows you," I interjected.

Allen was on fire. "Look, I said I don't know that girl. I saw her one time at a jewelry spot in Manhattan and we were introduced. That girl don't know me and I don't know her! She can go ahead with all that other shit."

Marlon joined in: "Man, these damn rappers be bigger groupies than the regular damn groupies."

We all laughed. Marlon's joke relaxed the tension in the room and we were back on track for a delightful evening. Danae's disruption was out of line, but at least it had produced the evidence that I needed.

The minute Danae and Marlon disappeared, it was on and poppin'! I undressed slowly, feeling his eyes caress every part of me, until I was down to my sexy little pearl-white thong and bra. His body was sick! Lean, with perfect muscles, and natural cuts. He stood naked by the edge of the bed and looked damn near edible. In a matter of seconds I was completely naked and my legs were wrapped around his back.

He stopped suddenly and asked, "Why Nas ain't marry you yet?"

I wasn't sure how to respond. "Well, if he did, I wouldn't be here with you right now."

"True," he replied with a smile.

We indulged in four rounds of carnal sexual pleasure that night and kept pace through the weekend. I felt very safe in his presence, especially after that night at the Palladium. I was wide open. But I never lost sight of reality, I knew without any warning all of this could end.

Back in New York, I dropped off Danae, then called Mrs. Jones to tell her I'd be over to pick up Destiny. Nas answered. He'd gotten home from tour while I was with Allen. He asked me to get a hotel suite and said that he and Destiny would meet me there in a few hours. This was normal for us, since we lived rather far away. I went home and packed a few things for Destiny and me, then checked into a suite by LaGuardia Airport. Nas arrived about an hour later.

"Where's Des?" I asked. I was nervous as hell.

"She fell asleep, so I left her at my mom's crib," he responded.

"Oh, I wanted to see her. I miss my little Nana." One beat too late, I added, "I missed you, too."

"Where were you this weekend, Carm?"

"Huh? Oh, I told you that I was going with Danae to her family reunion barbeque in Pennsylvania." I couldn't even look him in the eye.

"Why couldn't I reach you on your cell phone?" he asked. Then he flipped. "You wasn't in no fucking Pennsylvania with Danae. Who were you with, Carmen? Just tell me the truth and I won't get mad." It was too late, Nas was beyond mad.

After about an hour of intense interrogation Nas rolled up a blunt, smoked and calmed down. My nerves were so wrecked at that point that I even took a few puffs.

Nas started taking off his clothes. I was ready for anything but sex! But I couldn't reject him, so I went along with it. I pretty much knew the routine. Whenever Nas returns from the road, the first thing he wants to do is make love, then talk. In the middle of our session, Nas caught a crazy attitude. "Something doesn't feel right," he complained.

"You're right, something doesn't feel right." I went right along with it. I turned over, snatched the covers, divided the bed by making a crease with my open palm and rolled over, pretending to have an attitude as well. Nas and I didn't speak for the rest of the night. At first I felt somewhat guilty, but then I rewound and relived the wonderful weekend that I had just had with Allen. Surprisingly, Shawn ran across my mind. I wondered how he was doing and made a mental note to call him in the morning.

The next morning, I woke early. While Nas was asleep, I carefully and quietly dragged his jeans into the bathroom. Once inside, I went through his pockets, located his cell phone and scrolled through the contacts until I came across Foxy's number. "Got it."

After I'd dropped Nas off at the studio and put Destiny to sleep, I grabbed the cordless. It was time to make a phone call. When Foxy picked up, I launched into my verbal assault.

"This is Carmen. Look, bitch, I don't know what your problem is, but you don't know me, so stay the fuck out of my business."

She sucked in a breath. "What the fuck are you talking about?"

"You know exactly what I'm talking about. What do you have to gain by telling Nas anything about me and Allen Iverson? Bitch, you don't even know me and as a matter of fact you don't even know Allen."

"I do know Allen," Foxy claimed. "He—"

"No, you met him," I cut in. "There's a difference."

"Well, I told Nas that you were probably just a one-night stand and not to sweat it." Foxy's voice dripped with condescension. "And you're right, I don't know you, so I don't owe you shit. Nas is my nigga."

"One night?" I laughed. "Bitch, you wish you could get one call, let alone one night. Stay out of my mix, bitch."

Click! She hung up on me, but I didn't feel the need to call back. She got the point. Foxy immediately told Nas about our conversation.

"Carm, why would you stoop to her level?" he asked. "You are supposed to be bigger than that."

"Fuck her!" I explained.

"Carm, she's a lonely, insecure little girl," Nas said. "This bitch likes anybody who shows her a little attention. Anybody! Me, Jabari, Wiz. No one takes her seriously."

No matter how badly Nas and I were beefing, we could always relate as friends. We always came together to put the world and all its crazy inhabitants in their proper perspective. We'd been together for so long there was an underlying trust that no outsider could breach. Sometimes we'd get information that didn't add up but we always ended up decoding people's true motivations and strategizing the best course of action. This solidarity against outside forces convinced us our relationship was okay.

• • •

Weeks later things seemed to be back to normal, whatever that was. Nas was in and out of the studio and I was raising our daughter. Yet something was bothering me. Was I missing Allen? No—the truth was I missed Shawn. I wanted to reach out to him, but decided to play "wifey" and stay put. Nas was still on my back about my trip to Pennsylvania with Danae that never occurred.

One evening while doing laundry, I picked Nas's pants up from the floor and his pager fell out. As I viewed the numbers on the small screen, I could hear Nas running up the steps. He was returning for his pager. I quickly grabbed the phone, picked a random number from the pager and dialed. A chick answered! By this time Nas had entered the bathroom. I handed him the phone, still holding the pager. Nas looked puzzled but nevertheless took the phone.

"Hello, who's this?" he asked.

I snatched the phone from him. "How do you know Nas?" I asked.

The chick evasively described a business venture on which she and Nas were collaborating. Nas's face went scarlet with humiliation and his eyes began to light up with rage. I knew which emotion would prevail. Nas grabbed the phone and hung up. A rumble was coming. Before he could swing first I pulled out my pepper spray from my back pocket and sprayed Nas down like he was some rabid pit bull. The spray took Nas by surprise, yet despite his coughing and wheezing, he managed to grab hold of me. My instincts kicked in and I took advantage of having the upper hand. The fight was on!

I wrapped Nas's QB chain around my fist and tried to rip it off his neck and continued to whale on him. Nas's friends Wiz and Spud came running into the bedroom to break things up.

I just kept on swinging. When I finally tore Nas's QB chain off his neck, the fight was over. Nas coughed his way out the door, screaming, "You are fucking crazy!"

After he left I opened all the windows and aired out the house. As crazy as things had just been, I managed to get the place back to normal before picking up Destiny. If I could help it she'd never see any signs of her parents' conflicts. Nas called my cell phone and cursed me out. He claimed that I was a nut and needed psychiatric help. Although Nas was culpable in so many ways, this fight was my bad and I had made a complete fool out of myself. I apologized and we agreed to meet in front of Rennette's building.

When I arrived at Rennette's, Nas got in my car and we talked for a long while. We agreed to go home and put the fight behind us.

• • •

It's been weeks with no word from Allen. Then he finally called to announce that he had relocated to Philly. I couldn't wait to see him. Nas was leaving for Los Angeles the following day— that's when I'd make my move. Before leaving for the airport Nas asked for the QB chain I had won in our fight.

"Carm, stop playing, give me my chain."

"Nope, you can't get that back."

"Come on, Carm, stop fucking playing, give me back my fucking chain," he screamed.

I don't know why I refused to give him back his chain. I guess that was my way of maintaining some sort of victory over Nas.

That was the only power I had over him and I wasn't quite ready to give it up just yet. But Nas wanted that chain. He was nice for a couple of days in an effort to win it back.

"Carm, I'm going to L.A. I need my chain," he'd plead.

"Nah, you can't get that back," I said with a smile.

"But, Carm, I thought we made up. Why won't you give me the chain?"

I shrugged.

"Give me my fuckin' chain!" he yelled.

"Nope."

He ran upstairs to our bedroom and searched frantically through dresser drawers. He'd never find it. I'd hidden the chain in the basement behind the washing machine.

The following day Nas left for L.A. I confirmed my plans with Allen and started packing for the weekend. I wasn't expecting any visitors, so when Shelly and Jabari showed up at my front door they took me by surprise. I figured they were there in an attempt to recover Nas's chain. Jabari knew he didn't have a chance in hell with me, so he was actually wasting his breath. I grabbed my pepper spray and stuffed it in my back pocket, just in case I had to use it on Jabari. Shelly asked if she could speak to me in private, so we went to my bedroom and I listened as I packed.

"Carm, you need to give that boy back his chain. The rumors out there are really serious, and it's not making Nas look good at all." There were rumors circulating that someone snatched Nas's QB chain.

"Oh well, Shell. He is not getting his chain back! He should have thought about that before."

150

"Before what?" Shelly laughed. "Come on, what are you really going to do with that chain? Why are you thugging your baby-father out right now?"

"You know what, Shell, you're right. I'll only give up the chain because it's you. I wouldn't hand this over to anybody else."

"Thank you. Now Jabari will get off my back!" She laughed.

A few hours later, Rennette and I hit the highway. The two-hour ride was pleasant as well as therapeutic. Allen was waiting in his driveway when I arrived. I did my best not to blush at his big smile. When I entered the house, it was clear from all the shouting that he had a few friends over. After I was introduced to everyone, I took a mini tour of the place and it was lovely.

The entertainment room consumed the entire lower level: there was a pool table, a bar, and an enormous console TV with all types of Playstation games and electronics. I relaxed right away and got busy enjoying Allen's company.

When Allen and all his friends left for the game, Rennette and I stayed behind. I was always afraid to join him in public for fear of exposure. To entertain ourselves we went snooping around. Rennette was the bolder of us and she was the first to find the goods.

"I found something, Carm!" Rennette came out of Allen's bedroom closet squealing.

"What is it? What the hell is in there? Wait, put that back, I don't want to know, I changed my mind," I cried.

"No way, I just climbed all the way up to the tippy top of his fucking closest. We are gonna see what's in this damn box."

Every guy has a shoebox of love letters, photos and memorabilia, the closest you'll come to seeing a record of the notches on his belt. There was a love letter from a certain famous female

R&B singer—she was feelin' him! But there was also a photo of a girl who was damn near a midget. From eighteen to eighty-eight, from pencil-thin to chicks of Jabba-the-Hut proportions, there were all shapes and sizes in there.

I spent the next few days enjoying Allen's company. Another weekend with Allen was just what I needed.

CHAPTER 13

Awakening Carmen

· · · · · · · · · ·

THE WEATHER WAS CHANGING and my creative juices were starting to bubble. It had been a long time since I'd worked in the industry and it was time to get focused again. After having my daughter I found my perspective on things had changed, including my feelings about school. My rebellion against my mother was past and I was finally in a place where I was making all the decisions for my life. When classes started at FIT I went to school part time while my grandmother watched Destiny. Nas couldn't find me half the time because I was always on the go. I loved my new classes and it felt good to be doing something creative and productive. However, I began to really miss Shawn. It was time for him to come off punishment. I believed he was the one responsible for the rumors about us. When he answered the phone, all I could do was laugh. He called himself letting me have it.

"Where the hell have you been? And what's so funny?" Shawn asked.

I couldn't help but laugh.

"You, silly. I know you're the leak," I hissed.

"What are you talking about?"

"The rumors. You haven't heard the rumors going on about us?" I asked.

"Nope." He could barely contain his laughter.

"Well, now I have to give you a nickname."

"Like what?" he laughed. "Boo? That's a girl's favorite nickname for a nigga."

"No, not boo, that's too common and too corny," I said. "Okay, let me think of a nickname. SC. That's your new name, short for Shawn Carter. But I'm the only one that can call you SC."

"Okay, I love it," he said.

"Now, give me a nickname," I demanded. "And be creative."

He thought to himself for a moment. "Shorty, you my little shorty."

I sucked my teeth. "Ugh, you are so corny."

"Okay, okay, how about booberry. Like the cereal."

"That is the stupidest nickname I've ever heard!" I cried.

"Too bad, that's your new name!" he joked. "But seriously, Carm, I wanna ask you something. What's up with your boyfriend?"

"What do you mean?" I asked.

"I spoke to Biggie earlier," SC said. "He said he saw Nas at the Beverly Center and a nigga ain't even say nothin' to him.

He said Nas was comin' up the escalator, looked him dead in his face and ain't say shit. What's up with that?"

"Well, why didn't Biggie speak to Nas?" I asked. I always reflexively sided with Nas no matter how estranged we were.

"Carm, the nigga is on crutches, he was just in a car accident," SC said.

"Oh yeah, that's right." I sighed.

SC jumped back in. "Big just kept saying, 'Yo, Jay, do you know this nigga Nas didn't even speak to me? How this nigga gonna see me and not speak?' Carm, he couldn't believe he was so hurt behind that."

"SC, this is all news to me. Let me see what I can find out."

Biggie and Nas had no real history as friends, but had clicked instantly. Big would call like, "Hey Carm, you have that baby yet?" "Nas taking care of you?" In fact they each had no qualms about borrowing money from the other from time to time.

That night I asked Nas about the Biggie episode, though I naturally obscured the source of my information. To be safe, though, SC and I had worked up a story that he and Rennette were dating to avert any suspicion.

When I asked, Nas sat down heavily on the corner of the bed and looked a little dazed. "It's true," he said.

"So why didn't you speak to him?" I asked.

"I don't know, Carm. I mean, this fucking industry got me so caught up right now, I don't know why I just didn't say something," Nas said.

"Biggie was so hurt, Nas. I'm not saying you two were the best of friends but you were friends. When did that end?" I asked.

"Why didn't the nigga say what up to me?" he protested.

"Nas, he was on crutches, what was he supposed to do, hobble over?"

"Damn, I should've went over there. I feel fucked up but what can I do about it now?" he muttered.

It was the first time I heard Nas admit he might be caught up in industry politics. It was better late than never.

• • •

SC and I got closer over the next few months, despite periodic timeouts. We spent so much time on the phone that I began to consider him one of my best friends. We could talk a million times a day and the conversation would never go stale. Every time Nas and I fell out, SC would call. Like an angel in disguise, he always seemed to appear when I needed him the most.

We still hadn't had sex. We fooled around and SC definitely tried but I really didn't want to ruin the best friendship I'd ever had with a man. SC became jealous of whomever he thought was also checking for me. When Puffy released a song involving a girl named Carmen, SC called immediately to find out if I was seeing him. He also frequently asked about the Allen rumors.

But there was no doubt that we were slowly moving out of the friend zone. I stopped by his place one December day when I'd been out Christmas shopping. We watched television for a while and then went to his bedroom, where we laid down and smooched like sixth graders. When I refused to take things further, he reached over for his shoebox of love letters that was sitting on his bedside table. It wouldn't do SC any good to hide his shoebox up on a high shelf, as Allen did. He needed quick access to evidence of his sexual desirability, probably to persuade himself as much as potential conquests. SC started to pull out a few letters. I suggested he give me a massage instead.

"How does that feel?" SC asked, as he pressed his thumbs up against my shoulder blades.

That's a good spot," I sighed. "Your hands are so soft, do you get manicures?" I teased.

"Yeah right," he laughed.

"No I'm serious," I said, sitting up and warming to the topic. "Everything about you is just so well kept. Your do-rags look like you send them to the cleaners. I mean, you even have baby wipes in the bathroom! Come on, SC, what is that all about? Ugh, you are so vain!" SC had enough of my mouth and tackled me to the bed. He kissed me senseless and we played a bit more before it was time to end my short but sweet visit.

Over the next few weeks I noticed that I had gained some weight. Also, my period was late. I took a pregnancy test and it concluded that I was indeed pregnant. *This can't be happening,* I thought. This situation was serious, especially considering the fact that I hadn't been using protection and was sleeping with more than one person. I called Rennette in a panic. I tried with everything I had to maintain my composure.

"You're not going to believe this, but I'm pregnant, and I don't know who the father is," I cried. I was literally falling apart. Rennette was very supportive and insisted that I do what was best for me. From now on anyone that I slept with would have to use a condom, including Nas. In the meantime I had a situation that I had to take care of.

After the procedure, I went home and slept for hours. I was a mess, mentally as well as emotionally. The guilt was incredibly overwhelming. The following week I went to the pharmacy and purchased a box of condoms, intending to get in the habit of using protection. When I told Nas about the new rule, he wasn't too thrilled and insisted that I was overreacting. "Well, what's the problem, Carm? Why do you want to use condoms now, out of the blue?" he asked.

"Nas, I'm just not ready to have any more kids right now and I want to play it safe. We need to work on our situation first before we have more children," I explained.

That night while in bed, Nas started to feel a little frisky. When I pulled out the box of condoms, he huffed and puffed, but eventually put it on. Things were off to a good start and then all of a sudden Nas just stopped. "Carm, something doesn't feel right. I'm taking this condom off." After Nas removed the condom his erection went limp. There goes that. Then he started breathing heavy and said he was feeling a burning sensation. "Maybe you're sensitive to this brand. You'll be fine." I turned on the shower and told him to relax. He showered, but still wasn't relieved.

I ran back into the bedroom, took a look at the box of condoms and noticed that the box had expired over a year ago. Oops, my bad. Nas was on fire! The pain was getting worse by the minute and nothing seemed to be working. Finally I ran down to the kitchen and grabbed a cup, added warm water and a pinch of baking soda and returned to the bathroom. I put Nas's penis in the cup of water and told him to sit back and soak. I felt so sorry for him. I could see the discomfort in his facial expressions. It was at least an hour before Nas and his manhood were back to normal. "The things you put me through, Carm," he sighed.

On Christmas Eve day, Risa called to say she'd heard a rumor that Nas had been robbed on Jamaica Avenue after getting a haircut. I couldn't reach Nas on his cell so I called his barber at the shop who said that right after Nas left they heard some shots. It was ridiculous how fast the news spread. I felt like I was going to pass out. The thought of losing Nas had never hit home so hard before. I couldn't imagine life without him. I started to panic and didn't know who to call first. I couldn't think straight. My fingers were furiously paging him over and over with no response. All I could do was take Destiny home and wait for Nas.

Finally he came home. "Thank God, Nas. Are you okay?" I rushed over to him as he walked in the door. No blood on him, that was good. No gauze bandages either.

"Yeah," he said with a feigned offhandedness.

"Well, what happened?" I asked.

"I was coming out of the barber shop, up to the Coliseum parking lot. This dude was on the ramp and he came up and pushed a gun in my side and the nigga was talkin' to me like he knew me. "Nas, it ain't personal but it's the day before Christmas and I gotta do what I gotta do." So I grabbed the gun. I mean, Carm, me and this nigga were strugglin' for the gun and the next thing I knew the shit dropped and I just took off. That shit was so crazy, yo, I can't believe that shit just happened."

"Then what happened to the guy, where did the dude go?"

"Yo, I don't know, all I know is I was outta there."

My only response was wrapping my arms around him. Nas

could be a lot of things but I never had come so close to losing him before and it made me realize how much I really loved him. We weren't perfect but he was mine and I didn't want to live without him. That night we stayed together as a family and watched TV while the lights from our Christmas tree blinked. It was such a peaceful contrast to what Nas had just been through.

The very next week, Nas went back to the barbershop. He had something to prove. If he hadn't he would be tried again.

• • •

By the spring of 1997, the money from *It Was Written* was pouring in. Nas bought a brand-new black Mercedes V600 and a white Ford Expedition with the biggest wheels I'd ever seen.

He would also come home often with jewelry, bracelets, and furs for Des and me. Not to mention the cash he would drop on us. Some nights after performing Nas came home with pillowcases and shoeboxes full of money. He was good for blowing his earnings on ostentatious luxuries such as flying his barber to Paris to cut his hair for a show rather than having it cut before he left, or covering travel expenses for fifteen of his closest friends on tour.

This time I insisted Nas invest wisely. It was time to buy a house. While Nas was on tour in Europe, I searched for the best possible location and eventually found a pristine home in a gated community in Roslyn, Long Island. The exterior resembled a town house, though it was actually within a series of attached condominiums. We had five bedrooms, four bathrooms, a huge kitchen, a dining room and a sunken living room with cathedral ceilings. The upper level was a loft that overlooked the entire living space. The unit was absolutely beautiful, the best in the complex, and we had a fenced backyard where Destiny could play all day long. I was hoping the new atmosphere would bring our family closer together.

As we were moving into the Roslyn house, Mrs. Jones was spreading her wings in a garden apartment condominium that Nas had purchased just for her. Sha Sha announced a move herself: to Los Angeles. When I was younger we'd fantasized about moving to California, to a nice oceanside house with a backyard and in-ground pool. Sha Sha finally turned her daydream into a plan and put that plan into action. After she'd settled in Long Beach, Destiny and I flew out to visit her. A surge of good energy hit me as soon as I stepped off the plane. The air had a positive charge, the people were cordial and the temperature was just perfect. Sha Sha's one-bedroom apartment was so cute, a facsimile of the set for the TV show *Melrose Place.* This was the happiest I had ever seen my mother in a long time. We went shopping, decorated and did some sightseeing. It was nice to reconnect with Sha Sha, since I'd not seen much of her in the past year. I left Long Beach knowing I would one day move to California myself.

• • •

Even though Nas and I had just bought a new home in Roslyn he was back to his old tricks. He had no time for us. This just gave my friendship with SC a better opportunity to grow. So when SC called and invited me to his new apartment in New Jersey, I accepted without hesistation.

When I arrived at the address the first thing I noticed was the elegance of the building's exterior. It was a luxury high-rise, similar to the Jeffersons' Upper East Side building. A white-gloved doorman courteously directed me to the elevators. On the way I passed an in-house dry cleaning service with its own storefront. I laughed to myself.

SC greeted me at the door of his condo.

"Look at Jackie O. What do you think you're doin'?" he asked.

"I'm incognito," I said, removing my super-sized shades. He gave me a hug and kiss and led me inside. "You're so paranoid you're going to get us caught."

"I can't be too careful," I said, glancing around his bachelor's pad, which fit him to a T. "This is nice, SC." We walked over to the couch and sat down. "It's been a while. How long?"

"It's been three months," he said softly. "I missed you, Carm. You can't keep staying away from me for so long."

"I missed you too."

He nodded. All of his teasing finally got to me and I decided to break our rule and actually go out for once, so we went to a Chinese restaurant. It was well before the dinner rush and the place was nearly empty. There was no one around to recognize SC and no one could have possibly recognized me, since I refused to remove my sunglasses in the restaurant.

We ate and chatted throughout dinner but halfway through I couldn't resist teasing him. I took my sandal off and slid my foot up his leg and rested it in his lap. SC laughed. "Umm, looks like we are not going to make this movie."

Clearly the movie we'd planned was out of the question. We

wound up back at SC's place in front of the tube, holding hands and talking. After we kissed and dry-humped for, like, ever, SC tried his luck.

"Don't even think about it," I warned.

"Come on, Carm. It's been, like, a year. When are we going to do the freshie?"

"The what?" I asked, trying not to burst out laughing. "What did you just say?"

"The freshie," he repeated, as if I knew what the hell that meant.

"SC, what the fuck is the freshie? Where do you get these things from? The freshie? Booberry?" I laughed.

"Okay, when are we going to do it? Is that better?" He chuckled.

"When I'm ready."

"When are you going to be ready? Don't you know me well enough already? It's been a year. Come on, Carm, you can't be serious. I know a lotta dudes ended up leaving you alone just because of the wait. And I know they was feeling you as much as I do."

His transparent manipulation was exasperating. "First of all, we'll do it when I say we're going to do it and that's if we do it. Second, you're not going anywhere, because you've already invested the time. Like you said, it's been a year. Third, those same dudes that left because they couldn't wait don't know what they're missing. Maybe you will one day. Maybe!"

SC was silent. I could have sworn I heard crickets. I assumed I had shut him down and leaned back onto the couch. Seconds later his hands were back up my dress, pulling at my panties.

"Stop being fresh, SC. I'm not even playing!" I enjoyed the friendship we had built over time and didn't want to complicate things. When a woman is intimate with a man, especially one whom she genuinely cares for, she can't help but catch feelings. I wanted him, but refused to give in.

But SC was persistent. Every time I pulled my panties up, he pulled them down. Finally, I bolted off of the couch and ran to the back bedroom. He chased me all around the apartment. It was cute. I ducked into the kitchen, not realizing he was in there, and jumped on the counter.

"What did you do that for? Where are you going? In the cabinet?" he laughed. Then he pushed my shoulders down and jumped on top of me. It felt like it was getting ready to go down. I had to think quickly.

"We can't do it, you don't have a condom," I said.

He immediately stopped. "I'll be right back."

He got off the counter and disappeared. I didn't intend to have sex with SC, but now he was on his way back with a condom. I jumped off the counter and ran out on the balcony. He finally caught me in the bedroom and threw me on the bed. I was giggling the whole time. He was holding me down with one hand and fidgeting with something with the other. I caught a glimpse. He was putting on a condom.

"Stop, SC!" I wasn't giggling anymore.

"Why? What's the problem?" he asked.

"If you recall, I said you didn't have on a condom. I didn't say to get one."

We kissed some more and as we lay there with our bodies

flush together I could feel his erection at my entrance. I felt the tip just barely enter me. "Stop, SC!"

SC became very still. He looked me dead in the eyes. "Do you really want me to stop?" he asked.

"Yes."

"Okay," he said, and rolled off me. SC had a little attitude and took a seat on the floor, pretending to watch television, his pout making his lips even larger than usual. His forehead was as wrinkled as a man's twice his age. Just ten minutes later he was back in the bed laughing and joking with me. I appreciated SC's efforts to maintain his self-control; it really showed his respect for my wishes and that meant a lot. His willingness to restore our usual good humor and get things back to normal was a testament to his character.

After that night it seemed like SC and I were magnets. Over the next few months, just about every time I went out, we bumped heads.

Nas had a show on my twenty-sixth birthday, which freed me to celebrate the occasion with my closest friends. I knew the perfect spot for my birthday dinner: Justin's, Puffy's new Caribbean and soul food place. The morning of my birthday SC called.

"Happy birthday," he said.

"Who's this?" I asked jokingly.

"It's Sha with the burgundy Cherokee," he replied, raising his voice to disguise it. "What's up, shorty?"

"Stop playing, SC, I know it's you." I giggled.

"Wassup? What are you doing for your birthday?"

"Nothing much, just going to Justin's with my friends."

"I should roll with ya'll," he joked. He and I both knew that wasn't realistic.

"I'll call you later," I told SC. "When me and the girls finish dinner."

We got to Justin's around 9 P.M. All six of us looked ravishing, more edible than anything coming out of the kitchen. I wore a white fitted Gucci top, jeans, boots and a black hooded fox fur jacket. All eyes were on us as we entered the restaurant and were escorted to a table. Moments later the waiter, who was a familiar face to me, brought over a bottle of Cristal.

"John, you work here?"

"Yeah, just started," he said nervously. "The champagne is for ya'll."

My eyes surfed the room. "Who sent it?" I looked the room over a little more and spotted SC, who was smiling at me.

"Jay-Z," he said, shaking like a leaf. "Carmen, what is going on?" he screeched.

"Never you mind, John."

It would look bad if I were rude, so I excused myself and walked over to SC's table with stares burning holes in my back. SC was having dinner with his friends Dame Dash, Rhonda and another friend, Mike Kyser, who'd worked with me at Def Jam. Rhonda's presence helped to defuse the tension and also gave me a cover. "Hey Carm, wassup? Where you been?" Rhonda asked, giving me a hug. I chatted with them for a minute and returned to my table.

As I walked over to rejoin my friends, their faces all wore the same expression: "Hello, explanation!"

"An old friend from Def Jam sent the bottle," I explained. My lie seemed to satisfy everyone. Every now and then SC would motion for me to go to the ladies room. I shook my head. No way. Luckily my friends were telling jokes and didn't notice my sign language session with SC. He finished his dinner and even stopped by our table to take photos of us on his way out.

SC liked to play dangerously, but the risk was such a turn-on. Even knowing that he couldn't be fully trusted, I still couldn't help myself.

After we finished SC's Cristal, we went on to the next bottle and the next one, until I ended up drinking so much that I didn't even remember how I got home. I do remember Nas calling all night long to make sure I wasn't having too much fun. He never once wished me happy birthday.

CHAPTER 14

Escape from New York

· · · · · · · · ·

ANOTHER CHRISTMAS ROLLED IN and I did my usual shopping, cooking and decorating. The fun part was that Destiny was now old enough to help out. She got a real kick out of helping me cook and decorate. By this time, Nas and I were fighting regularly. His gripe was that Destiny and I were never home. He claimed I was changing, and he was right. Nas was never home anyway, so I made it my business to keep busy, otherwise I would have gone crazy. Even if it was a trip to the park, Destiny and I were there. We did everything together. Wherever I went, she was right there.

Clearly, Christmas bombed thanks to Nas. The mood was totally ruined. He was like a real live Scrooge. I tried to maintain for Destiny. I wanted her to be happy and didn't want to take away from her day. So I just ignored Nas.

New Year's Eve was certainly not going to be spent with Nas. I wanted to bring the new year in on a positive note. I called SC early that morning from Risa's house. We were both on the same page and made plans to hook up that evening. I got to his house at around 11 P.M. After we settled we toasted to the new year and sat on the couch and talked a bit. The mood was very relaxed, no hype, very simple and intimate. We started kissing and it was rather intense. Somehow we ended up in his bedroom. He started to undress me and this time I didn't resist. My clothes were off in a flash and so were his. When he leaned in, I suggested immediately that he get a condom. "Don't move and I mean it," he said as he dashed into the walk-in closet. It had been a long wait. The time before didn't count. When he returned that's when the lovemaking began.

We kissed, and I moaned as he penetrated me. He was huge. Initially, I didn't have any expectations because the first sexual encounter is always awkward for both parties. So I wasn't shocked by his physical performance. It was quick, but I was satisfied. The sex was passionate and sweet. Then he gave me another one of those mind-blowing massages. "Damn, why did you make me wait so long?" he asked. I just smiled. I had to make sure that his intentions were in the right place. We both drifted off to sleep in each other's arms.

• • •

"Good morning!" SC said, smiling, buck naked and holding a glass of fresh-squeezed orange juice. I giggled at his naked antics. I loved the fact that he was so free. It seemed like we had grown even closer after we made love. In a nutshell SC was like my homie, lover and friend. The more time we spent together the fonder I grew of him. We jumped in the shower. As I lathered up, SC began to perform a strange action. With his legs slightly bent, he held a washcloth with both hands at either end and slid the cloth up and down the crack of his butt.

"SC, what the hell are you doing? Playing the violin?"

He looked up. "What? I'm washing my butt."

"That's how you wash your butt?"

"This is the last time I take a shower with you!" He laughed.

I got out, toweled off and went back to the bedroom. As SC came out of the shower, I was double-checking my neck for hickies in the mirror. Now it was his turn to make fun of me. "You are really paranoid," SC said.

"Just checking," I replied.

"What would happen if you went home with a hickey on your neck?" he asked.

"Me and Destiny would be knocking on your door looking for a place to stay," I replied with a smile.

"Ya'll could come, but not like that," he confirmed.

I started to notice a pattern with SC. He would never fully reveal himself or what he was truly feeling. Like most men, he kept his true feelings bottled up. It didn't shock me in the least bit, that's just who he was. Deep down I knew that SC really wanted me to leave Nas and be with him, but he was too insecure to admit it. He lacked a great deal of confidence. We both desired the same things, but we knew it could never happen. I wasn't afraid to leave Nas, but I was afraid to leave him for SC. The truth of the matter was that I was more concerned with how Nas would take such a blow. He would have been devastated. I wasn't afraid of what Nas would do to me, but what he would do to himself or SC, for that matter.

SC and I enjoyed each other's company and conversation. He often invited me along to shows and concerts. Though I would have loved to go with him, especially since I'd waited so long for Nas to invite me on such occasions, I always had to say no. Our time together was very private.

Although SC's celebrity status was increasing, my interactions with him remained the same. I'd still go over to his place, kick off my shoes, go in his closet, get an undershirt, and watch movies with him. Our times together were like vacations from real life. However, SC was always on borrowed time. Nas's time.

Rumors intensified about SC and I. Things got crazy at home, with Nas constantly probing me about the gossip.

One evening Paul called. I hadn't spoken to him or anyone in Connecticut for so long. I was excited to hear from him, but soon found out that he was calling with some bad news. Casual got nabbed by the feds. They were watching him for a while and their persistence eventually paid off. I was heartbroken by the news and made plans to meet Paul in Harlem later that evening.

After I got dressed and ready to go I noticed that my pocketbook was missing. I couldn't find it anywhere. I finally called to Nas, who was in the bathroom, asking if he had seen my purse. The bathroom door opened. Nas was holding my bag. He tackled me to the floor and pinned my arms down.

"Nas, get off, you're hurting me."

"Who are you fucking with, Carm? Just tell me the truth." Nas's face was beet red and his nostrils flared.

"Nas, what are you talking about?" I screamed as I tried to break free of his hold. But he was sitting on my stomach. I was trapped.

"Carm, who are you going to see uptown?" he yelled at the top of his lungs. Then he spit in my face.

I was crying and could barely speak. "I hate you," I bawled.

"I hate you too," Nas replied. He got up and left.

I called Paul and told them him I had to take a rain check. I don't know exactly what happened next. It was as if I went mad and lost control over my emotions. There was no outlet for my anger but the house itself. I tore the place apart, went to war using the objects on hand. I got the broom and smashed everything in sight. I threw one of my favorite vases across the room where it landed on our glass coffee table, leaving it and the table in pieces. The neighbors called the police. When they arrived I told them that I was home alone watching a movie and would turn the volume down. Nas came in a couple of hours later, viewed the results of my fit and walked back out the door. What else was new?

• • •

A few weeks later the SC rumors had reached their peak. Tracey even called and said she had heard about SC sending a bottle of champagne over to my table that night at Justin's. Things got crazy, especially at home. Nas was probing me about the new rumors. *What am I doing*, I thought? I called SC. When I barked on him about the rumors, he suggested that I play dumb. "If you don't give him no info, he won't know shit, Carm."

"Tell me something I don't know." I didn't need SC to school me on how to deal with the rumors. What I needed was a reality check! I saw myself as the same person that I'd accused Nas of being. I then began to question some of my own actions. How did I let myself get to this point? Everything Nas and I had gone through wasn't totally his fault. I'd contributed to the problems a great deal. I was now ready for a change. I knew that I was capable of having much more substance. It was time to evolve. Destiny was growing and I didn't want to keep exposing her to all the chaos. Our relationship was dysfunctional and unhealthy. I had to do some serious soul searching.

I decided then that Destiny and I were moving to California. I wasn't sure when we'd leave or where we'd live. I just knew that we were moving. I called SC a few days later and told him I was moving to Los Angeles. His blasé response suggested he didn't take me seriously. He offered me his whole-hearted support and wished me well. "You should follow your heart," he said.

The next evening Nas and I went to Mr. Chow's for dinner. I broke the news as gently as I could.

"Nas, you know I love you, right?" I said softly. The restaurant's soft lighting was bringing out Nas's eyes, making it harder to say what I had to say.

"Yeah, and I love you too boo."

"I know you do. But see, I'm ready to move on. I'm leaving you. Destiny and I are moving to California."

The silence was deadly. Nas let out a light chuckle. "What are you talking about? Now what's the problem?"

"I'm not happy. I've had enough, and I'm ready to move on."

"Carm, you're wildin' right now," he said, affecting a calm tone. He picked up one of the overly sweet chicken dumplings that the waiter had insisted we just had to order. "Just relax, nobody is moving anywhere. Let's just go on a vacation, just you and me. We can work all of this out."

"It's too late. I've made up my mind. I don't want to be with you anymore."

"Hold up! You don't want to be with me? Do you know how many women would love to be in your shoes?"

I slipped my heels off underneath the table and offered them to Nas. "Here. Size five. They can have them."

Nas jumped up from the table, paid the bill and stormed out of the restaurant. I put my shoes back on and called a car service to get home.

Over the next few weeks, Sha Sha helped me make arrangements for the move. "I knew when I moved out here you were going to follow behind," Sha Sha said over the phone, happily pretending to complain. "I can't go nowhere without you."

Before I left, I went out with my girlfriends for a big blowout farewell. On the drive home, Rennette and I had a heart to heart. She was one of my best friends and I would truly miss her. After we got through all the mushy stuff, Rennette seized the opportunity for a final face-to-face dishfest.

"I've always wanted to ask you something," she said. "Who's better in bed, SC or Nas?"

"Well, to be honest, they are about the same. Nas is an average size, but he's a freak! SC is way too conventional for my taste, but he's huge and also very passionate. So if I had to rate them, I would give them both the same score, but for different reasons."

"Okay, what do you mean SC is way too conventional?"

"You know, like boy on top, girl on the bottom. Nas is different. Nas will do anything I tell him to. We be doing home videos and everything. I never told you about the time I caught Wiz watching one of our sex videos, did I?"

"Bitch, what happened?" Rennette asked eagerly.

"Well, one night after Nas and I finished having a big fight, we made up and filmed ourselves. Ever since, we've been making videos. That's just something we enjoy doing. So anyway, Nas got in late from the studio one night and he brought Wiz home with him. When I woke up the next morning, Wiz was at the kitchen table with the video camera. When he saw me he froze. At first I thought, 'Oh he's up early, maybe I startled him.' He asked me to call him a cab. So I called him a cab and after he left I went back into the kitchen. When I noticed the video camera on the table, I picked it up to put it away. Then I noticed the tape was at the very end. So I rewound it just a little and viewed it. I could not believe what I saw. It was one of our home videos! This nigga was up all night watching our X-rated video. I was on fire! So I ran into the bedroom and told Nas what had happened. He got up, called Wiz and went ballistic on him. He stopped speaking to Wiz for like a month."

Rennette's mouth was wide open when I finished telling the

story. There was a pause. We both erupted into laughter at the absurdity of it all. I could tell Rennette anything. Would I find friends like her in California?

The movers arrived early on a February morning. My belongings were boxed and ready to go. Nas was stressed. He hadn't taken me seriously and now it was too late. The load was light; I had packed mostly clothes and very little furniture. I planned to purchase all new things when I got to California. *New furniture for new beginnings,* I thought. Nas wore this blank look on his face. He was speechless. He didn't know what to say or do. Even his physical gestures were very awkward. He couldn't sit, stand, lean, anything. How could he control this situation?

"Carm, please, don't leave. We can work this out. Let's just go on vacation, spend some quality time together and make this work." Nas had underestimated me. He thought I was weak and incapable of taking such a huge leap of faith.

That morning was dreadful for all of us. I could see the hurt in Nas's eyes. It had been nine years, and now it was over. I explained that what we had was special but that it was now time for us both to move on. I told Nas that it takes two to make things work and ended by saying that I had no regrets. There was an awkward silence, which clearly told me that he still didn't get it.

CHAPTER 15

City of Angels

· · · · · · · · · ·

THE ICONIC HOLLYWOOD SIGN stood tall in the smoggy air. I gazed at the cityscape, already loving California and all the possibilities it had to offer. I had previously found a pre-school for Destiny as well as an apartment, which definitely made things easier once we arrived. There was so much to think about. After we'd spent a few days hustling around and tending to our basic needs, the movers arrived, and we unpacked and settled in. I rolled around on the carpet of our empty new home and cried while thanking God for all his blessings.

Nas seemed to call every other minute. I couldn't understand where all the concern was coming from. When we lived together in New York, I couldn't hold Nas's full attention for more than five minutes before he was off with his friends. Now when he called he'd try to convince me to move back to New

York. It wasn't going to happen. I had a new plan now. Destiny was adjusting to Los Angeles smoothly. She jumped right into the swing of things at school and I was delighted to be in my new zone, meeting new people and feeling free as a bird. We had a routine, just like we had in New York. I would take her to school in the A.M., do my entire running around and pick her up. Then she and I would either go to the park, the library or get a bite to eat. Destiny and I always had quality time together. I looked into furthering my acting technique and enrolled in classes at the Margie Harbor Studio. It wasn't long before I found an agent and started auditioning.

A month after we arrived my cousin Hasan moved to L.A. from Atlanta. I was so excited. Hasan was fun, loving and adventurous. And just like me, he was also a risk taker. We both made the decision not to lose track of what we were trying to accomplish and leave foolish play to the unwise, but things turned out differently. This was the second time that he and I had been on a journey together.

The first time was back in high school when Hasan decided to form a female rap group. Of course his position was to play the back. But I couldn't rap! We called ourselves BWP, which stood for Bitches With Problems. Hasan knew that I couldn't rap, but he insisted that my look was marketable, so I just went along with it. Our image was supposed to be a hard-core group, but my delivery wasn't giving off that impression. I sounded more like Molly from AT&T customer service or something. I just wasn't making the cut. We hung in there as long as we could, but the group eventually broke up and that was the end of my rap career.

Now it was time to embark on new business ventures. We were still young and vibrant individuals looking for real opportunities. That's when I started exploring the filmmaking business. I would create the master script and of course would be cast as a principal. I had it all figured out.

I spent a lot of time at Hasan's house, conveniently located off the Sunset strip. With no traffic to fight, we were always two minutes away from the action. We were both feeling out the whole Hollywood thing. L.A. was very different from New York. New Yorkers are very conscious of their appearance whereas people on the coast were more carefree and laid-back. This was an exciting period. Nas even bought me a brand-new Mercedes Benz S500 in horizon blue. Rick from Power Motors picked it out and had it shipped. Although I appreciated the gift and gesture, I knew it was merely a desperate attempt on Nas's part to get me back. He was trying so hard, but going about it the wrong way.

Now the only thing missing was a connect. That's when I met CJ, a low-key weed dealer who couldn't have come at a better time. I needed my treats and he was only dealing with top quality stuff. He came highly recommended by Redman and I was always happy with his product. Eventually he became a part of the family. I was delighted.

One morning after dropping Destiny off at pre-school, I got a call from Risa, who had just spoken to SC. SC was shocked to hear about my move.

SC picked up on the second ring.

"Hey SC," I said, trying to sound extra bubbly.

"Don't hey SC me. Where you at?"

"I'm in Cali."

"How did you get out there? What happened?"

"SC, I told you that I was moving months ago."

"I guess I didn't take you seriously."

"You're not the only one."

"Wow, I can't believe you just up and left without telling me. I always thought . . . well, never mind." I knew what SC was thinking. He had assumed that if I left Nas I would do it to be with him. "Are you happy?" he asked.

"Yes, and I absolutely love it out here in Cali. My mom is out here, Destiny is loving it, so yes, I'm very happy."

SC took a deep breath. "Well if you're happy, then I'm happy."

• • •

Not long after we moved out to L.A., Nas called one evening while I was bathing Destiny. "Hey, I'm at Puff's house in Malibu," he said. "We're about to have dinner and he's sending a car for you and Destiny."

"Oh really, who's idea was that?" I asked.

"It was Puff's idea. I told him that the fam was out here and he said, 'Cool, I'll send my driver to get them.' "

Fifteen minutes later, Puff's driver was at the door. I wasn't quite finished bathing Destiny and had to get us both dressed and ready. An hour later we were at Puff's house in Malibu.

"Why did it take you so long?" Nas asked.

"We had to get ready, Nas."

"But it's been, like, an hour. We had to go ahead and eat."

"Leave it alone," Puff said. "They're here now, it's cool. Are ya'll hungry? I can have my chef fix you anything you like."

"No, thank you, we already ate," I replied.

The beach was close enough that I could hear waves pounding the shore. Such a soothing sound to live by, every wave a fresh start. Puff's backyard looked and felt like a Caribbean island: tropical plants, mellow lights. Inside, he had the finest furniture.

"If You Had My Love," J.Lo's first single, was playing on repeat. Puff's significant other was in the living room and appeared to be just a down-to-earth, around-the-way girl wearing dark jeans and a ponytail.

Destiny shyly stuck to me like a magnet on steel. While I was talking to Paul Hunter, a video director, I noticed Puff eyeing me. There were complete paragraphs of shameless suggestions in every glance. I gave him a loaded look in return. Then I caught myself. What was I doing?

Back at my apartment later, Nas asked, "Carm, did Puff ever try to talk to you?"

"No!" I answered.

"Are you sure?"

"Positive," I answered with my fingers crossed.

. . .

After being in L.A. for a few months I noticed that Nas was often in my new town. Business trips surfaced out of nowhere. He would take care of business and be back at my place by nightfall. I felt like I was back in the same situation all over again. It wouldn't have been so bad if Nas opened up and we addressed things that we disagreed on, but he never wanted to talk. One night, I just came out with it.

"Nas, we need to talk. I can't do this anymore. I only see you when Destiny is in school or asleep. This has got to end. You should only come by to see Destiny."

"I'm out here taking care of business so that my daughter can go to private school and have a place to rest her head. Everything I do is for you and Destiny. I have no life without ya'll! I miss ya'll so much and I want my family back."

I missed Nas just as much as he claimed to have missed me, but not enough to return to the same situation. I was, however, very homesick for New York and missed my friends and family. That summer Nas flew Destiny and me to New York frequently. During one visit, SC called. For the life of me I couldn't figure out how he knew that I was back in town.

"How did you know I was in New York?"

"I know everything that you do. You got in last night. Now get ya little ass over here. I want to see you, bad!"

"I'm going to have to pass. This is really not a good time," I whined.

"All I know is, ya little ass better be over here tomorrow, and I don't want to hear no excuses," he demanded.

I couldn't figure it out at first, but eventually it came to me. Steve Stoute. Steve was SC's messenger. Was he playing both sides of the fence? Nas would tell Steve all his business, and all my business. Could that be how SC knew my every move?

The following afternoon, SC and I had a private picnic. I was so excited to see him. When I arrived the apartment door was cracked, as usual.

SC came out from the bedroom and snatched me up, lifting me off my feet as he squeezed me tightly. For some reason I had butterflies in my stomach. I couldn't believe I was nervous. What had come over me? Was it that we hadn't seen each other in a minute? After a couple of drinks I was back in my comfort zone. SC and I made a nice little nest on the floor of his master bedroom and got comfortable. There was never any frontin' behind closed doors. We shared the entire afternoon watching television, talking, laughing, and making love.

There was no rush to go back to L.A. and I had some catching up to do with friends and family, so Destiny and I ended up hanging around the Big Apple most of the summer. Toward its end Shelly called and wanted to hang out. Shelly is a party promoter, so she's pretty informed about the hot spots and you never know where you'll end up. It was about three o'clock in the morning when we got dressed and hit the town. I wasn't worried about Nas. We were no longer a couple and he was out doing him, so I was out doing me. But when we got to the Roxy I noticed a familiar black SUV parked across the street.

"Shelly, is that Nas's new truck?" I said.

"No, that's not his whip," she replied. So we went on in. It was packed! After being inside for about two minutes, I noticed SC at the bar. I walked over. He immediately grabbed me and gave me his usual bear hug. Then I noticed he was acting sort of odd and peculiar. His eyes were roaming the room, scanning the crowd as if he were looking for someone.

"You are going to cause some trouble up in here tonight,"

he mumbled. I just smiled. He let me go. "If you don't have any plans, let me take you and your friend out to breakfast."

After the club let out, SC called my cell phone and we made plans to meet at a diner near his place in Jersey. We linked up about a half hour later. He brought Ty Ty with him. Shelly and Ty Ty had already met and he'd had a big crush on her for years. After breakfast we all went back to SC's house.

SC was coming up and it was starting to show. His penthouse was even more posh than his previous dwelling. The apartment was absolutely beautiful. It was obvious that he had just moved in, maybe even that very day. SC was pretty drunk, so I knew it was going to be a good night. When SC is inebriated his stamina increases tremendously. By the time I had undressed, SC was buck naked on the floor and under the covers. I slowly mounted myself on top of him. After about thirty minutes, SC exploded, and passed out. I got dressed and woke up Shelly, who was asleep in the living room. We bounced.

When the liquor wore off, I beat the hell out of myself for having failed to use a condom! What was I thinking? Just a few months prior, I was back in L.A. preparing for a family vacation to Jamaica when I noticed an unusual discharge. At first, I brushed it off with the thought that perhaps I'd developed a yeast infection. But I wasn't convinced because yeast infections were abnormal for me. After three days of speculating I went to the GYN. After the exam, the doctor called me into his office and explained that I had a vaginal infection that was transmitted through sexual intercourse. "What? You have to be kidding me. I have an STD?" I was in total shock! I knew STDs were a common and dangerous problem but it wasn't until then that

I realized how careless I had been not protecting myself. This was the risk of not being in a monogamous relationship. I felt angry and irresponsible. And, to make matters worse, I wasn't sure who gave it to me.

After I left the office, I called Nas and went off on him! I cursed him out like a sailor, calling him every name in the book, then hung up on him. The trip was off! That was it! There was no way I was going anywhere with Nas, not after he burnt me! For the next days I refused to take Nas's calls. We were finished as far as I was concerned. I didn't want to hear shit.

Eventually I came around and we spoke. "Let me speak to my daughter, where's my daughter?" Typical Nas. After I let Des speak to her father, it was clear that he had just informed her of the trip cancelation. Her little face looked so sad, and she had these little puppy dog eyes that were staring up at me in disbelief, like I was the bad guy! She handed me the phone and that's when he let me have it. "You dirty bitch. I didn't fucking burn you, you better check that other crumb nigga you fuck with! I'm clean as a whistle. I can't believe you!" I was stuck! But now we had *new* drama! The thought of SC giving me an STD really upset me. I didn't know what to believe. I never found out where it came from.

I was fucking pissed!

When I got to Long Island, Nas was still asleep in bed. He woke up furious.

"Where were you at all night, Carm?"

"Shelly and I spent the night at Risa's after we hung out at the Roxy for a minute."

"Word, I was there and I didn't see you, or Shelly."

My heart sank. So that's why SC had said, "You about to cause some trouble up in here tonight." SC was playing with fire. That was a close one! It was almost as close a call as Mariah Carey's New Year's Eve party the previous year. Nas and I had been huddled in a corner all night when SC spotted me and came over with a bottle in his hand. He couldn't see Nas! As he approached I was trembling and sweating, thinking that night would be the night it was all exposed. SC finally noticed Nas and took a detour just in time. But now SC didn't seem to be willing to take detours anymore, and even seemed to want to create a head-on collision with the truth. I was glad to be heading back to L.A. It was definitely time to go.

CHAPTER 16

Hollywood High

. . . .

OUR SUMMER ENDED WITH a severe downpour. The morning started off pretty badly and we had sort of a chaotic departure. We woke up late and had to rush to the airport. The rain didn't help matters. But Destiny and I were heading back to California and I was so relieved. It was time to get back into our routine. The nasty weather made saying goodbye to my hometown that much easier. It definitely felt like the fall had arrived, a bit prematurely considering it was still the last week in August. We took our regular flight on American Airlines, and departed JFK at 9 A.M. and landed around twelve. This was perfect. It gave me enough time to prepare for school the next day, fix dinner and spend a few hours with Destiny. Destiny would be starting a new pre-school at Wonder Years and I planned on diving full speed into my acting career.

When we got home, we unpacked and I whipped up something simple to eat. Spaghetti! Destiny and I ate dinner, I gave her a bath and we were both in bed by 9 P.M. Destiny was excited about her first day. Wonder Years was a small pre-school on Sepulveda Boulevard. Miss Debbie was Destiny's teacher. She was about 5'7", in her late thirties, slim with dusty blond hair. She was very pleasant and always wore a smile. Of course all of the furniture was very small. It was so cute. A hallway zigzagged through a maze of cramped cubbies where the children placed their personal belongings. There were workrooms where an assortment of games, coloring utensils, rubber mats and everything you could think of in a nursery was neatly in place. There was so much fun stuff crowding the nursery that there was no room for anything else. When the weather would permit, the children played outside in the sandbox or on the sliding board, teeter-totter and swingset. Destiny had no apprehensions about running off to play with her new classmates so I knew she was comfortable in her new surroundings and that put me more at ease.

I was loving life in L.A.—the weather, the people, the walks to Starbucks. I loved everything about Los Angeles, and wanted to stay. It was time to get started on my screenplay. Nas became a resident of California himself. He was officially bi-coastal. He rented a pre-furnished cozy little dwelling located on Santa Monica Beach about five minutes away from us. Nas insisted that his move was beneficial to his career, but I knew better. He was slowly working his way back into creating the same situation I had left behind in New York. His presence made me feel stagnant. It was difficult to digest. On the other hand, I couldn't blame him for moving to L.A. L.A. was the bomb. Maybe it wouldn't be so bad after all. Just maybe we would be able to work things out.

In the meantime, I wasn't feeling myself and it had nothing to do with Nas. I tried to sleep it off, but after making my sixth obligatory stop to the bathroom before 5 A.M., I realized something was wrong. I was vomiting profusely and felt lightheaded. Did I catch a bug? Had I come in contact with something viral? I wasn't sure, but I knew I wouldn't be able to take on my daily activities. I dropped Destiny off at school, stopped at Dunkin Donuts to get my usual—a medium hazelnut coffee, light and sweet, and then proceeded home. I hadn't completely entered the door before puking all over myself. I felt feverish and faint. I was even having hot flashes.

What was wrong? Where was all of my energy going? Later that evening Destiny and I sat down for dinner and I still wasn't feeling right. Destiny noticed it immediately in my eyes. She reached across the table and gently rubbed my hand. "Mommy, do you feel okay?" she asked.

"I'm just a little tired, Destiny," I replied.

"Maybe you ate something bad today," she continued.

"Maybe you're right! You know me so well, Destiny," I replied.

"We have to take care of each other, right?"

"Yes. We do." That was so sweet and innocent of her. Her little face always warms my insides with comfort. I love my little Des.

The night progressed and still no change. I was still vomiting and feeling horrible. The remnants of Chicken Piccata over rice pilaf with mixed steamed veggies had exploded all over my toilet. I fell to my knees in front of the bowl and held on for dear life. Afraid to let go, I kept one hand around the seat cover and with the other, I wet a wash cloth and dampened my face. Destiny was still sound asleep. I was thankful that my drama wasn't disturbing her. Could I be pregnant? Oh, Lord! I hoped not. The first thing to do was to get a home pregnancy test.

The next morning I dropped Destiny off at school and went to a local pharmacy to purchase a home pregnancy kit. I returned home and took the test, and waited. The suspense was eating me alive. The first pink stripe had appeared in the first window. Now it was a matter of the second stripe appearing in the second window, which would determine my pregnancy. At a snail's pace, the line became visible. "Oh, no!" I was pregnant and it wasn't Nas's! We'd been using protection ever since that little STD incident. What the hell was I going to do? I knew right away it was SC's. A quick flash of that hot summer night at his new penthouse ran through my mind. A part of me was excited and the other part of me was disappointed. I was battling with the old Carmen and the Carmen I aspired to be. Under the circumstances, I knew that as much as I wanted to, there was no way I could go through with the pregnancy.

During the next few days I did my best to maintain my normal regimen. I continued to go to the gym, even though it took everything I had. By the third day, I was completely worn out. The very next morning when I woke up I knew something was dreadfully wrong. As I got up to go to the bathroom, I noticed that I was soaking wet from the waist down. When I turned on the light in the bathroom, I was shocked at my discovery. My lower body was completely covered with blood. I just knew immediately that I was having a miscarriage. I undressed and jumped in the shower. Although I was extremely upset, I was very quiet so that I wouldn't disturb Destiny. I knew that Destiny would have lost her mind if she saw me covered in blood.

After dropping her at school, I went to the GYN. He concluded that I was having a natural abortion. I was sad, yet a part of me was relieved. I felt a sudden urge to call SC. For some reason I felt like as the father he had a right to know. At first he was quiet. "Hello, SC, are you still there?" I said.

"Yeah, I'm here, I was just thinking about something. So are you okay, is everything all right?" he replied.

"I'm good," I said.

"Wow, I told you I was going to get you pregnant, see?" he went on.

"Yeah, you said that a few times. The things you do, SC."

We spoke for a little while longer about life, love and true happiness. He made it clear that we were in this together and everything would work out for the best.

Each day, Nas questioned my whereabouts and of course, whom I was dealing with! Then he started screaming and carrying on about a number he had found on my dresser. When he showed me the number, the name read CJ. I nonchalantly said, "That's the weed dude, Nas. You are playing ya-self." He was so worked up and I wasn't in the mood, so I ignored him while he accused me of sleeping with CJ. He was fuming. I kept quiet, which made his boiling temper even worse. Then he swung, striking me in the face with an open hand. Then he grabbed me and shoved me into the refrigerator. For the first time ever, I didn't fight back. I was trying to be a new person. If I didn't let myself be abused, Nas couldn't play the abuser. Nas was thrown off and confused by my non-reaction.

During the chaos, my cell phone continued to ring in the background. Whoever it was really was trying to get hold of me because they would call, hang up, then call back again.

"Who the fuck is that blowing up ya cell, Carm," Nas barked.

He was in my face, foaming at the mouth. I managed to get out of the kitchen and grab my keys and bag as I fled my own apartment. I was so grateful that Destiny was in school.

Once I got in the car, my cell started ringing again. It was SC, he was here in L.A.

"What's up shawty? Whatchu doin?"

Typical SC, always there to save the day.

"Hey, SC!" I replied. "Can you hang out? I want to see you." I was exhausted, still furious with Nas and could use a quick pick-me-up. I told SC that I was a little hungry and to meet me at my favorite Spanish restaurant, Fried Bananas, on Santa Monica Boulevard. Because it was in a predominantly gay neighborhood, I knew there was no chance of running into Nas. I got myself together in the car. I pulled my hair into a curly ponytail, added a little gloss and some pressed powder and tried to cover up any evidence of a recent physical altercation. I was good to go.

A bleached blonde dressed in a uniform two sizes too small approached the table and greeted us with menus. He was tanned and wore a beautiful smile. Typical Californian. This place had the best food. SC and I sat side by side at a booth in the back. I was so happy to see him. He and I moved closer together as his hand slid between my knees. SC could never keep his hands off me, and he knew I secretly enjoyed it. I ordered chicken and yellow rice with black beans and plantains. SC claimed he wasn't hungry, but ate from my plate once the food arrived. I didn't mind. I told him about my new business venture with Risa. "SC, I need a favor," I said.

"Sure, anything, what is it?" he replied.

"Well, I need you to do a song for the soundtrack. I was told that if I presented a tight soundtrack with the script, I'd have a better chance at securing a deal. So can you do a song for scale?" which meant 2G's flat.

He just looked at me puzzled. "Scale?" he said. "Carm, I'll do it for free." Then he pulled me even closer to him by the waist and started licking my earlobe. Now I couldn't keep my hands off him. We were all over each other. When the waiter returned with the check, I could read his mind: "Take it to a hotel, please!" After a wonderful lunch, SC resumed doing what ever it was that he was doing and I went back to my apartment.

Before I could reach home Nas called and apologized for his actions. "Carm, I'm so sorry. I will never ever put my hands on you again. Will you please forgive me?" I forgave Nas, and he kept his word. He never laid a hand on me after that.

• • •

Nas felt horrible and tried his best to make it up to me. He spent more quality time with Destiny and me and even started bringing us with him on his business ventures. Nas had just dropped his fourth album, *Nastradamous,* and was filming his video at a studio in L.A. Destiny and I went along and pretty much stayed in the trailer. We were there for hours. When we got back to my place later that night, I went searching through Nas's pants and found a folded-up piece of paper with Beyoncé's number on it. Like I said before, old habits are hard to break.

When I questioned Nas about the number, he said that Beyoncé and Kelly flew in to appear in the video. He went on to say that Beyoncé had a little crush on him and wanted to hook up before she flew out the next morning.

"So, why didn't you get up with her?" I asked.

"'Cause, Carm, I mean, she's a pretty girl and everything, but she's mad young and I got respect for her pops. Mathew is my man and we are working together," he replied.

"Pretty sure. What is the real reason? Beyoncé is the bomb!" I questioned.

"Well, to be honest, I can't take her breath. Yo, Carm, her breath is off the chain," he said, laughing.

"Well, your breath ain't always peaches and cream, Nas!" I rebutted.

"Yeah, but I'm a nigga. I can get away with stank breath every once in a while." We ended the conversation on a good note and retired to bed. A few days later, Nas flew back to New York.

• • •

That weekend, Michelle, Hasan's friend and roommate, invited us both to go with her to a barbeque. She was good friends with

Larenz Tate and didn't want to go to the barbeque alone. She and Larenz met at an audition and exchanged telephone numbers. She too was an actor/model/dancer. Of course, Hasan and I went along for support and to check out the menu. When we entered Larenz's crib, it was all eyes on us. It was obvious most of the women there resented Michelle. She knew the majority of them. There was this eerie, unsettling feeling, like they wanted to jump her or something.

Larenz, on the other hand, was a great host. From the minute we walked in he made sure we were good. "Ya'll want something to eat, ya'll want something to drink? What can I get you?" he went on. His home was decorated stylishly with all the trimmings. It had a warm feel. Overall, Larenz's aura was very personable.

On the ride to the barbeque Hasan and I had smoked a blunt, so we were extra relaxed. I felt good on the inside, but the munchies were slowly taking effect. We sat at a table conveniently located by the food station. Everything looked scrumptious. The spread was unbelievable. There was fried chicken, barbequed chicken, burgers, potato salad, macaroni salad, fruit salad, the works. I got up and helped myself to a little bit of everything. Just as I sat down to eat, Larenz walked over and asked Michelle and me if we would be interested in going for a swim. We both declined. "What's the problem? You ladies don't have bathing suits? If that's the case I can send someone to get you whatever you need. What are your sizes?" he said sincerely.

"You're so kind, but no thank you," I replied. He turned and headed back over to poolside to join his friends. Two seconds later he returned and pulled Michelle to the side. I didn't bother to concern myself with what he wanted, so Hasan and I went for a second serving of food. I'd probably regret it later, though Hasan didn't worry much about his chunky frame.

Michelle joined us and was wearing a silly smirk.

"Spit it out, bitch! What did he say?" I asked.

"Carm, they want you to get in that pool bad. Real bad!" Michelle replied. I took a quick glance so not to give notice, but they noticed anyway. I didn't want to seem rude or nasty, but then again I didn't want to send mixed signals, so I looked down. There was nothing there but pavement. I could still feel their eyes on me, so I turned my head and continued eating. Nothing could persuade me to get in that pool. I was flattered, but flattery was not enough to get me in that water.

The day was slowly passing and the air was getting cooler. It was time to leave. The later it got, the more people showed up. Before leaving I gave Larenz a friendly kiss on the cheek and a hug and thanked him for his hospitality. It was an evening to remember.

The following week, I called to check on Sha Sha. She insisted that I read this new book that was referred to her by a close friend. The name of the book was *Conversations with God* by Neale Donald Walsch. After I read the book, I felt like I had made a friend in God, one that I never knew. I laughed and cried through the entire book. This was the book that literally changed my life. A huge burden was lifted and I became consciously aware of who I was and who I desired to be. I was growing and evolving, but yet had so many unanswered questions.

The more answers I received, the more questions I had. I realized that I had been neglecting my spirituality and God's guidance. I was so caught up in the physical world that I rarely took the time for self. That's when I started meditating. I had never taken the time to stop and listen. God speaks to everyone, but not everyone listens. I was now ready to listen! I knew then that the person I was (a liar, a cheater, a gossiper, etc.) was not who I now desired to be.

Through reading the passages in the book, I realized that my past experiences were all blessings in disguise. I had to first be who I was not, in order to be who I am. You can't experience hot until you've experienced cold. You can't know up unless you've been down. And you can't experience love until you've felt the wrath of pain, and vice versa. I came to know that in life people don't make mistakes, they make choices. After reading *Conversations with God,* I chose to accept myself and others without comment or judgment.

This revelation began a new season in my life. My new goal was to be the greatest and grandest version of the vision that I saw for myself. Don't get me wrong, it was easier said than done. Becoming a new person is a process. In the begining I would constantly fall short of the goals that I set. Especially when it came to Nas, who was at his wits' end trying to figure out a way to get us back. In a sense I began to feel sorry for Nas. He looked bad physically and it was apparent that he was losing it. Even though Nas and I were seperated, is was as if nothing had really changed and somehow, some way we were still connected and a part of each other's daily lives. When we were in New York, we stayed with Nas. And when he visited L.A., he stayed with us. The in-between times were filled with phone calls and two-way pages. It was as if we were still a couple. And of course we were still intimate.

. . .

Happy birthday! Destiny was turning five and I had planned a birthday party at her school. Hasan helped me prepare for Destiny's special day the night before. We stayed up half the night frying chicken, and making potato salad, cupcakes and grab bags for her classmates. I could see the excitement in her eyes. She looked adorable. She wore the cutest white sundress, with colorful flowers and white sandals. I put pink, lavender and purple beads at the ends of her box braids and let her wear a little gloss. Her beautiful smile completed her outfit.

When we entered her school she took special notice in a little boy and he reciprocated with a blush. It was obvious the two liked each other, but I didn't want to embarrass her or him, so I acted as if I never noticed. Miss Debbie and I decorated the tables and Destiny took her seat in the birthday girl chair that Miss Debbie had pre-decorated. The little boy took a seat right next to her. Destiny was so happy. The party lasted for about forty-five minutes and then it was time to get back to regular school activities. I left and picked her up a couple of hours later. After school I took her to Benihanas, her favorite restaurant, and we topped the night with a visit to Baskin-Robbins.

Because I was living in Los Angeles alone I didn't trust anyone with my baby. I got referrals for a lot of baby-sitting agencys and child care providers, but I couldn't and didn't want to take a chance on them. Sha Sha helped me a lot. Whenever I really needed her she was there to take care of her granddaughter. Sha Sha would have Destiny every other weekend and they would hang out in Long Beach. They frequently visited the malls and the beach. Wherever Sha Sha had to go, she took Destiny with her. Destiny always came back home singing a new gospel song.

One weekend while Destiny was with Sha Sha, Hasan called and said that he would be going to Vegas for a few days. After speaking with him briefly it was a done deal. Vegas, here I come. Hasan, his girlfriend, his cousin Sean and Sean's girl were cashing in their winnings at the Belagio Hotel by the time I arrived. Hasan had obtained a free coupon for a suite at the hotel for the weekend. All of the hotel expenses were covered. Hasan spent all of his time gambling. He loves the slot machines! I dropped my bags off in the room and went down to the casino. This was my first time in Vegas and I was loving it already. The strip was like nothing I had ever seen before. It was like a scene in the movies—the bright flashy lights, the people, hustlers, everything moved so quickly. It was so easy to get engrossed with the gam bling and lose sight of the fact that the drinks are free all night. Minute by minute you drink until you're past the point of intoxication, reaching a delusional state of mind, and then you're passed out flat on your back. We spent the rest of the evening gambling, drinking, laughing and "paying taxes"! That's a game where when someone hits the jackpot, everyone reaches in the winner's bucket really fast and grabs as many coins as they can. Gotta pay your taxes! When I would hit on the machines I kindly shared two coins with everyone.

The next day, we gambled and walked the strip. By nightfall

we were back in the casino. It was an instant replay of the night before. The following day we checked out of the hotel. Even though I had a round-trip ticket and the plane ride was only forty-five minutes, I took the four-hour drive back to California with Hasan and friends.

Christmas was right around the corner and I did my usual decorating and shopping. Whenever the holidays rolled around it was always stressful and sometimes disappointing. Nas would be flying in any day now and we would be celebrating our first Christmas in Los Angeles. The weather was beautiful. It was kind of difficult getting into the Christmas spirit without any cold weather or snow, but we tried. My birthday was four days before Christmas and it started off great. In the morning, Destiny and I ate breakfast together and then I dropped her off at school. SC called a few hours later to wish me a happy birthday. My Christmas spirit was picking up a little and I felt good. Nas's flight had landed early, December 21st, just in time for my birthday.

I welcomed him with open arms and gave him a big kiss. He held me so tight that it was hard to breathe, but I would have happily let him squeeze me to death. Then, he suddenly dropped down on one knee and revealed a small black box. My body was tingling. I almost started to quiver. Was he about to propose? *Oh, my God!* I thought. After all we had been through the time had finally come and to be quite honest, this was the furthest thing from my mind. I never in a million years thought that he was coming here to do this. He opened the box and I was speechless.

"Will you marry me?"

We'd always talked about marriage. Our first few months to-gether we fantasized about the ceremony we'd hold in my grand-mother's backyard, just like Sha Sha's wedding to Van's father.

"I'll wear a blue velour suit," Nas would say.

"Maybe you should wear white velour, Nas. It's more tradi-tional."

"Well, what are you gonna wear?"

"A pearl-white bustier," I'd always say. "With jean shorts, natu-rally."

And now, this was the moment I had been waiting for my en-tire life.

"Yes!" I cried. Nas stood on his feet, placed the pear-shaped diamond on my finger and we kissed and embraced.

So many questions filled my head, but I kept them to my-self. Nas and I both had done and said a lot to each other that could never be taken back. It was time to move on and wipe the slate clean. Wow! This was truly a special moment. We stayed at Hasan's for a short time, then picked Destiny up from school and went back to my place. I cooked dinner, put Destiny to bed, then cuddled on the couch with Nas while we watched *The Sixth Sense* on bootleg. The next day when we broke the news to Sha Sha she was blissful, but I sensed her reservations. I know Sha Sha wanted the best for me, but I also knew that she wanted me and Nas to finally get it together.

Weeks passed and the holiday spirit eventually died. Busi-nesses were open during regular business hours. School had resumed and I was getting back into the swing of things. Risa called me and mentioned that she had spoken to SC. That was fine because she and SC had that type of friendship. They were cool. She said that she told him that Nas had proposed to me on my birthday. SC didn't say a word, according to Risa. I guess he was shocked and had presumed that my relationship with Nas was over, but he was wrong.

"Hello! Hello, are you still there?" Risa asked.

"Yeah, I'm still here." Risa told me that SC had finally responded, "Word! I'm happy for her. Where she at?"

"She's still in L.A.," Risa had replied.

He wanted to hear it from me. This time I decided I would take my time. This was it for me and SC. I was going to marry Nas. Once I became Nas's wife, my relationship with SC would be dead, I mean dead and stinking. There would be no phone calls, no friendly chats, nothing. After some time I finally called him and broke the news.

"Hey, SC."

"So, I heard the good news. Are you happy?"

It took me a minute to answer that question.

"Yeah, yeah, I am," I choked out.

"Well, if you're happy, then I'm happy."

He seemed sincere when he said that he was happy for me, but I knew he was hurt. I could hear it in his voice. I agreed to see him one last time before Nas and I eloped in Vegas.

Nas and I made plans to catch a flight to Vegas and elope. But as fate would have it, the weekend we'd planned to go to Vegas, Destiny caught a stomach virus. She stayed home from school for the week, giving me enough time to decide that we shouldn't rush into things. It seemed like a sign: We weren't supposed to elope. A traditional wedding would be best, we agreed. I started planning and making lists of potential bridesmaids and guests. Deep in my heart, though, I wondered if our wedding would ever really happen. It seemed doubtful that we'd truly put the past behind us.

CHAPTER 17

The Beginning of The End

. . . .

MY PREMONITION OF A doomed wedding was proven correct
with the midnight phone call from Nas. "Tell me something,
Carm. Is he talking about you?"

He referred to SC's verse on Memphis Bleek's song, "Is That
Your Chick." When I finally heard the song, my response vacil-
lated between disbelief and anger. His disparaging lyrics gave no
indication of the solid friendship SC and I shared. I was pissed,
but this new attack on Nas's manhood brought out a deeper
emotion. Nas and I had practically raised each other from ad-
olescence to adulthood. I was the only one who deserved to
belittle Nas as a man. Especially after all I went through! Nas
deserved to have a fighting chance.

And I was naïve enough to believe the uncovering of my affair with SC would bring closure to my relationship with Nas. So

when Nas called me back the following night, I finally confirmed the rumors and confessed that I was indeed having an affair with SC and had been for five years.

"*Five years! Five years, Carm?* What the fuck is wrong with you? What was you thinking? You mean all this time I been hearing rumors about you and this nigga, brushing them off like, 'Nah, not Carm. She may do her thing but she would never disrespect me like that.' "

The very next morning I woke up with the worst headache, as if my brain was expanding and threatening to break open my skull. It hurt too much to get mad or even argue. Nas called, pissy drunk. His words slurred when he spoke and I could hardly understand him. I heard a lot of ruckus in the background so I figured he was in the Bridge.

"Carm, give me that nigga's address."

"Nas, come on, what are you really thinking right now? Don't ruin your life over some dumb shit. It happened, it's over. Now let's just move on. If you go to his crib, do you really think he's going to come outside? You're going to end up getting arrested and it's not worth it."

"I want his address," he repeated coldly. Then he broke down. "How could you? And with that nigga. Carm, how could you?"

There was no soothing him. In the beginning, I'd had my reservations about getting with SC, but the truth was I enjoyed his company, and he'd been a better boyfriend to me than Nas in recent years. I simply couldn't help developing feelings for him. I couldn't take back those moments and didn't want to. What's done is done. Now I hoped Nas wouldn't retaliate physically and do something he might regret later, something that might also jeopardize Destiny's future.

Nas slammed the phone down in my ear and headed over to SC's office. He called up and found Dame Dash at the office, but not SC. Nas insisted Dame come downstairs. But Dame refused, claiming his son was with him, and invited Nas to come upstairs instead. Nas and his goons retreated to the Bridge. I then called SC. No point beating around the bush.

"Listen, I told Nas everything," I said, as soon as he answered. "You wanted him to know about us. You've been dry-snitching in your songs all these years. Now he knows."

There was an ominous silence.

"Hello? SC, are you still there?" I asked.

"Yeah, I was just thinking about something. What did you tell him?" SC asked.

"I told him everything, from beginning to end. I heard the song, SC. You're fooling no one."

"What song? What are you talking about?" he replied.

"Whatever, SC. You know damn well what I'm talking about. 'Is That Your Chick.' Does that song ring a bell?" I barked.

"Carm, you can't be serious. Listen to the song. In no way, shape or form does my verse depict our relationship. Come on, Carm." He was such a cool liar. It was now time for "How could you think I would do something like that?"

"It is what it is," I said. "I thought I'd let you know. Nas is on a rampage and he already went up to your office looking for you."

"Nas ain't got it all and he's an emotional dude." For the first time since I'd known him, SC sounded worried. "And the niggas that follow behind him ain't got nothing to live for."

"I know, SC, that's why I'm giving you the heads up."

"Carm, do you know what you just started?"

"What I started? SC, I don't rhyme!" *Oh no,* I thought, *Please don't tell me this nigga is scared.* He fumbled his words and I could hear the fear in his voice.

"Hold up, SC. Let me find out Nas got you under pressure," I went on. His tone changed that instant. Out of nowhere, a burst of courage came through the phone.

"Whatever, fuck it!" he said with a serious tone.

"You always said that what's done in the dark eventually comes to light," I responded.

The conversation lasted for about thirty minutes or so and then he come out with "I want to see you so bad." And even with all the drama, I wanted to see him too. We were playing a dangerous game and we both welcomed the excitement of a forbidden moment. Even though I was totally pissed at SC, I agreed to see him a few days later. For me, SC had always been forbidden fruit. Seeing him now would be even more wrong, and more exciting. Risky and sexy. Impossible . . . and necessary.

But over the following days, Nas became so hysterical that I decided to fly to New York to comfort him. Nas was asleep when we arrived. I stood over him and watched him sleep. He didn't look too good. Even in sleep his unhappiness was evident: the furrowed brow, shallow breathing, his caramel complexion gone a little yellowish. Well, I thought bitterly, now the shoe is on the other foot. Maybe now Nas could see what he'd put me through with his women and long disappearances. As I watched Nas, I also thought of our good moments, especially the golden period of our relationship before Destiny was born. My compassion for Nas ran deeper than my revenge.

I hated seeing him like this. He needed my support and family was the key. Destiny and I stayed close by. Deep down I really think that he wanted me around to make sure that I wasn't with SC. Since Destiny and I had left for New York, I didn't see SC as planned. Nas needed me and I stayed right by his side. We stayed for a few days, then returned to L.A.

· · ·

I was doing my best to go back to my normal life in L.A. Nas had sold the house in Roslyn and purchased a huge mansion in Old Westbury, Long Island. The realtor told me that Nas hoped to win me back with the estate, to make up for lost moments with Destiny and me. Once again, he just didn't get it.

Early in the summer, Destiny and I returned to New York to visit friends and family. After the release of "Is That Your Chick" Nas's beef with SC had remained a private drama, with me absorbing the brunt of the hostility. The beef became public at the 2001 Summer Jam.

With the escalating Nas and SC beef, I knew I was living dangerously, yet there was some part of me that believed my affair with SC had nothing to do with Nas. At one time Nas and I wanted the same things. We were in the same book, on the same chapter, but on a totally different page.

It was morning when Risa paged me. SC had gotten in touch

with her and wanted to know what was going on. Nas intercepted the page and all hell broke loose. First Nas cursed Risa out, then he went off on me. "I hope you choke on diet pills." Risa was a little chubby at the time. "Carm, what is wrong with you? You still dealing with this nigga?" I didn't say a word. I knew he was going through a lot so I just took it. The next few days I tried my best to comfort Nas, but it was very difficult. The mood was constantly changing. One minute we were fine and the next we couldn't stand being in the same room with each other. I needed a break. I decided to go and spend time with SC for a few hours. I told Nas I was going to a friend's house. Even though I knew for sure that SC deliberately attempted to sabotage my relationship with Nas, I accepted the fact that he was human and was acting strictly out of emotion.

When I saw SC, I noticed he didn't make eye contact with me. That was unusual. Guilt and frustration masked his face and accented his every word. SC and I talked the entire time I was there. We both had a lot on our plates and had much to discuss. I told SC that now was the time to be who we claimed we were. I made it clear that things would only get worse if we allowed it to.

A couple of hours later, I entered the house and Nas was still in a bad mood. He was exactly the same as he had been earlier. This trip would be a short one, I decided, so Destiny and I headed back to Cali a few days later.

Days after I was back in Cali, SC flew out as well on business. A few friends and I went to a party and we bumped into him.

"Where you been? I've been trying to reach you," he said. I could tell he was drunk.

"I'm so bad with cell phones and messages," I said. SC wasn't alone, he was with Dr. Dre, Dame, Steve Stoute, Tone from Track Masters and a few other people. The minute I saw Steve warning bells went off in my head. Knowing Steve was there put a damper on my fun. I knew I had to be careful with my approach because I feared he was playing both sides of the fence. All he would need was a tidbit of information and from that he would produce an entire story.

When SC saw me, he lost it. He couldn't maintain his composure and was very touchy feely. I was on pins and needles.

"Chill out, SC, we are in public!"

"I don't care," he replied.

His hands were all over me. He grabbed my ass and was pulling me close to him. Steve stood directly in front of us with his mouth open and eyes glued to us. If he were a mirror I would have been staring at my own reflection, that's how close he was. We both froze. I had to do something. I dug my nails as hard as I could into SC's hand. SC was so stoned. The alcohol had him acting reckless and out of character.

I spun around and darted into the ladies room. The heat was on. Steve made sure to watch my every move. Minutes later I joined my friends. "What was that all about?" they asked in a huddle.

"Nothing. We'll talk later, right now I'm ready to go home!" The night ended with me getting home safely and passing out on the couch.

With all the drama, I knew I was living dangerously, but SC was still my friend and I couldn't stay mad at him. So when he called during my next quick stint in New York and invited me over, I couldn't help myself.

"*True Romance*, this is my favorite movie," I blurted when I saw it mixed in with the other DVDs on his rack.

"Word? It's one of my favorites too," he replied.

Aw, I thought to myself, *we're like the ghetto version of Patricia Arquette and Christian Slater.*

"Why don't you go to the liquor cabinet in the dining room and get us a bottle of wine," he suggested.

"No problem," I replied.

I went to the dining room cabinet and was faced with a huge collection of fine wines and champagnes. My eyes darted from shelf to shelf. There was a variety of everything. I picked a bottle of Chardonnay, but just as I was about to walk away, I noticed a bottle all the way at the tippy top.

Hum! I thought. *That must really be the good stuff.* The reach was too high, so I got a chair, stood on my tiptoes and grabbed it. Datcha 97! Ah ha! Chardonnay goes back. Datcha 97 is the pick of the evening. The bottle still had the price tag on the bottom. Nine hundred dollars. I climbed down, put the chair back and opened the Datcha. Grabbed two wine glasses and returned to the bedroom.

SC noticed the bottle in my hand and whispered, "Good choice."

"Pretty sure!" I responded.

We were halfway through the movie, when SC started to undress me. It was a heated moment and my insides were so warm. The wine had me buzzed. It was a lot smoother and fruitier than Chardonnay. I drank just about the whole bottle. I was so relaxed, but I had to remind myself not to fall asleep. I had to get back to Long Island. I had faint voices in my head reminding me to stay awake. "Stay awake, Carmen. Stay awake!" It would be hard fighting against the liquor but I had to pace myself. And this time we would be using a condom. By 2 A.M. SC was knocked out. I kissed him on the lips and bounced. I got home in forty-five minutes. Nas still wasn't home. I took a shower and got in the bed. A few minutes later I heard Nas as he opened the front door. He crashed right beside me. No words, no touching, just two bodies sharing a bed.

The days flew by with family visits and parties with friends, but L.A. was calling me home. Los Angeles was a breath of fresh air. I returned to the west coast in time for Destiny to start second grade. On her first day it was a rat race in the lobby of Page Private School. Parents were darting all over the place with their children. Destiny was my little trooper. She was at ease the entire time and actually couldn't wait for me to leave. I knew by the end of the day she would have a million stories about new friends.

A few days after my return I got an urgent call from Shelly. She informed me that Mrs. Jones had developed breast cancer and was growing severely ill. Shelly and Mrs. Jones were very close and she confided in Shelly a lot. So that's why Nas had moved his mother in with him; to be close in case something should go wrong. She needed her family together. This was all news to me, I'm not sure how long she had it. I wasn't aware of her condition.

On top of this there were great financial problems. The mansion was costing a fortune and Nas was hitting rock bottom. He was carrying a lot of weight. The mansion was just too much for Nas to maintain. The rooms were completely empty with the exception of the bedrooms and one of the living rooms. It was just a big empty house.

The months were sprinting by and it was now summer. Nas was broke, which meant that I was broke. It didn't really hit me until we had nothing. My younger sister Nini came to stay with us at the mansion for the summer. We had more than enough space so it was no problem at all. She and I took several trips to my brother Van's studio in Queens to keep busy. Destiny was off to camp early in the morning and we'd pick her up around 4 P.M. and head back to Long Island. Although we were on a tight budget, we made the best of it.

· · ·

Back in L.A., one particular morning while I was getting Destiny ready for school, the phone rang. I thought to myself, *Who could this be at this early hour?* It was SC. He was in town and wanted to see me. His hotel was literally five minutes away. After I dropped Destiny off, I picked up some whipped cream and strawberries and headed to SC's hotel. He kissed and hugged me, then he asked, "What's in the bag?"

"Oh, just a can of whipped cream and some fresh strawberries," I replied.

"What's that for?" he asked, excited.

"What do you think? Silly," I said.

SC rubbed his palms together and tightened his lips. We watched TV and cuddled for a while, but SC had his mind on other things.

"When are you going to get the whipped cream and strawberries?"

"Right now!" I replied.

By the time I returned to the bedroom with the goodies, SC was completely naked and stretched out on the bed. I got undressed and then decorated his frame with the whipped cream. I fed him a few strawberries, then got busy. As I licked his body clean, he moaned, all the while calling my name. We hung out for a couple of hours at his bungalow-style suite until we both fell asleep. I woke up about a half hour later and left to go to my vocal lesson.

Nas was aware of the fact that SC and I were still communicating. This disturbed him greatly because he was in New York and couldn't keep tabs on me. Even through everything that had happened, Nas never stopped wanting us back. When he realized that buying the mansion wasn't going to change anything between us, he wanted out. He started looking into purchasing property in Atlanta. He wanted an escape from New York. I considered the move and agreed that it might be the best thing for us all. A fresh start. Destiny was getting pretty lonely and wanted a permanent playmate, a sibling. She wanted Mommy to have another baby. In a sense I was ready to settle down. I just hoped that I could put everything behind us.

Maybe this was what was meant for me. Maybe it was meant for Nas and me to be together and it was time for us both to get it together. I still had a lot of love for Nas. More than anything in the world, I just wanted a family, a real family. Love could be right around the corner for us again. I could fall back in love if I just gave it another chance, I kept telling myself. I was back and forth with my emotions until I finally gave in. We were moving to Atlanta, would probably get married and have more kids.

A ranch-style home, something simple and something that we could call home, was waiting in Atlanta. I hadn't seen the house yet. It needed some work, according to Nas, and he wanted it to be a surprise. He described it as being pretty big, but simple with just a few bedrooms and full basement. All we had to do was build a pool in the back and it would be the perfect home. He made it clear that we would be living the simple life and I was fine with that. We could live in a mansion or a matchbox, as long as there was peace, I was with it. I started packing and making the arrangements. The days ahead were a countdown to our new lives.

As soon as we made our new plans, the rumors began to swell. "SC and Carmen are an item!" This was the word on the streets. Nas couldn't and didn't want to handle it. I think what bothered him most was that everyone else knew. His pride was on the line. Radio personalities were feeding the listeners with speculation and over-exaggerated stories. This was a rough time!

One particular afternoon Nas called. Something had to be wrong. Nas was out of breath and almost speaking in hysterics.

He was about to go on the air with Wendy Williams. Apparently Wendy was on the air going on and on about some X-rated video of me and SC. This was a rumor she had heard about. She even offered a $5,000 reward to the person who could deliver the tape to her as proof. Nas called the show. While he talked to her on the air he had me on the phone listening. She had him right where she wanted him. He completely made a fool of himself. At that point I was disgusted. He made our relationship seem like a one-night stand. He couldn't understand why I was on the other line breaking. He explained that he had to basically cover his ass! "Carm, what was I supposed to do? I can't let the public know what's really going on."

I was livid. "Nas, you made me seem like a groupie you met in the club and knocked up on a humble," I shouted. "If we are starting over, everything should be put behind us. We are planning a wedding, for Christ's sake, and starting over," I continued.

"I know, Carm and I want the plans to stay the same. I didn't know what else to do. This bitch was on the radio wildin' about a video this nigga Jay got."

"There is no video, Nas," I said. "You played yourself! And now there is absolutely no way we'll ever be together."

I cancelled everything. There was going to be no reconciling. It was a done deal as far as I was concerned. Nas would always uphold his image above his family. He gave his all to the industry, so the industry could have him. Now Nas had another dilemma on his hands. He had a house with no family to share it with.

Papa Lenny called after hearing Nas on the radio and was

pissed. "I knew Nas was a sucker. Man, that nigga played his-self." Papa Lenny was beyond upset with Nas, but even more so with SC. He wanted to know who he was and where he could be found. I had to sugarcoat the situation and explain to my father that these were the things that happened in the industry. I went on to say how unfortunate it was that it had to happen this way and how weak my baby-father was. After speaking with Papa Lenny and giving him a rational explanation it was time to give SC a call.

I was upset. I was fine until I spoke with my father, but I couldn't let this go on without addressing SC. I asked him, "Is there something you want to tell me?" He denied Wendy's allegations. He swore that there was no video. I had to hear it for myself. Deep down I knew there was no video. SC wasn't that kind of nigga, and I knew for sure that he was too insecure to do a porn himself. He would be exposing his sensitive, sexual side to a vast majority. No way, no how! So I wasn't worried about a video. I was more concerned with where this whole thing was going and more important, where it would end. I started crying, I was so upset. I tried to hold it in but couldn't. This was the first time SC had ever seen this side of me. I broke down on the phone. Everything just caved in on me all at once.

My father was one thing, but what if Sha Sha heard this. I was more worried about my parents and Destiny. SC offered to handle the situation before it got too out of hand. He reacted to Nas's sheepish reply to Wendy. "Why did ya asshole boyfriend call that bitch? What is wrong with him?" After we talked some more he said, "You know, Carm, I always thought that you and me would have a baby and get married." I sighed and brushed it off. Enough game already. I responded with "Whatever, SC." I was too emotional at that point. We ended the conversation. I pondered over everything and let it all digest. I was not getting back with Nas, that was evident. Nas was who he was and he wasn't changing. Nas and I had to accept each other for who we both were and that could be done separately.

CHAPTER 18

All Eyes on Me

· · · · · · · · · ·

THE FOLLOWING DAY WENDY read a fax on the air that she received from SC stating that the allegations regarding the X-rated video were untrue and he apologized to my father and family for any distress that may have been caused as a result of false information. At that point Nas felt even more threatened by SC and was fuming with rage. After all, SC had just saved the day. He wanted SC's home address and was willing to do what he had to do to get it. After refusing repeatedly, Nas used Destiny's child support as collateral. I couldn't believe he was doing this. The checks had stopped! Things had changed drastically and our lives spiraled downward.

If that wasn't enough, one morning after I dropped Destiny off at school, the steering wheel of my car suddenly took on a life of its own. Luckily there was a service station on the corner.

I pulled in, but didn't have money for repairs. What was I going to do?

A kind stranger drove up behind me in an old Land Rover and emerged from his vehicle and asked if I needed any help. He introduced himself as Wood Harris. He was tall and dark with diamond-shaped eyes and an energy that tickled my spine. He smelled like a fresh shower and shave, and wore sweats.

"How you doing? I noticed that you were having some trouble with your car. Is there anything I can do? Do you need a ride or something?"

"No, I think I'll be all right, but thanks," I replied.

I called AAA and they picked up the car, which was fortunately still under warranty. The Benz dealer even arranged for a rental to be dropped off at my house that afternoon. Wood invited me over to his house for lunch the next day and I happily accepted.

As I walked up to his small, villa-style home, I was greeted by a friendly German Shepherd in a red bandanna. Wood opened the door and graciously showed me around, pointing out the studio where he painted and wrote music. Throughout the house the air was sweetened with sandalwood incense.

We spent the rest of the afternoon at his kitchen table talking about poetry, politics and our children. We found that we had a lot in common. He loved animals and music. He played a few pieces on the guitar for me and I was impressed. He talked about the movies he played in and a new series he had just auditioned for, *The Wire*. We ate lunch. He had prepared some frozen organic brocolli and nut muffins and in less than five minutes the food was done and we were eating and drinking tea. It felt great to be around someone as free and spiritual as I was. He was like the male version of myself. His relationship with his son's mother went sour some time ago and fortunately the breakup didn't interfere with the relationship he had with his son. He spent every weekend with his son and Thursdays as well. He also picked his son up after school every day. I had found a new friend. Wood and I spent every day together after our impromptu introduction. We would drop the kids off then meet back at his house. I loved going to his house. We spent our mornings in front of the TV. He came along at the right time and was just what I needed. He was a good friend.

Wood was the perfect distraction from all the bullshit. Nas and I were barely speaking and when we did, all he would say was, "What is this nigga's address, Carm?" I couldn't take it. Nas was worried about all of the wrong things.

In the meantime my rent was two months in arrears, the cable was off and Destiny's tuition was overdue. Her school called daily for payment.

But my financial troubles worsened, and by November we were being evicted, the phone was disconnected, my cell was about to get cut off and I was in a real mess. I had to seriously evaluate everything. The only option was to enroll Destiny into public school, but that would mean relocating all over again. I had no choice but to move back home to New York. I called my grandmother the next day and explained the situation. And of course Grandma, being Grandma, welcomed her grand and great-grand with open arms. All I had to do now was find the resources to get back to New York.

I looked in my jewelry box. Many pieces glimmered with value and flashed the suggestion of good money. It was hard to decide. As I closed the box, something glinted on my left hand. My engagement ring! Why was I still wearing it? It was no longer a symbol of love or commitment. I headed to Beverly Hills, where pawn shops are almost considered lending institutions. A store there would have the cash to buy a valuable piece of jewelry.

The shop display included antique silver, gold bracelets, emerald rings, Cartier watches, and furs—yep, I'd come to the right place. The owner greeted me warmly but gave me a strange look when he took the ring. He hunkered down over my engagement ring and scrutinized it thoroughly. He looked up. "It's a fugazy!" he said with a sick laugh. He showed me. It wasn't a complete fake but certainly not worth the money Nas had paid for it. He offered me twenty-five hundred and I took it.

Destiny and I flew to New York and settled in Queens at my grandmother's house. Our stay there was brief. When I called Nas to let him know of Destiny's whereabouts, it was as if he had turned into a new man. Nas apologized repeatedly for his rash behavior. He made arrangements for me to fly back out to L.A. to retrieve my engagement ring and then spent a lot of time with Destiny and me.

He begged me to move into the mansion with him. I did because I felt like I had no choice. The schools were better, not to mention I had no job and a daughter to feed. I enrolled Destiny in school in Old Westbury and agreed to come back to Long Island on a temporary basis only. With Destiny accustomed to private California schools, the culture shock of a Queens school would have put her into early therapy.

I also made it very clear to Nas that we were not a couple and our relationship was open. Destiny was thrilled with the living situation. She had her mommy, daddy, and Grandma Ann all living together. Mrs. Jones was always a big help when it came to Destiny.

• • •

I was broke, depressed, and eager for a change, so I started looking for a place of my own. I knew it was just a matter of time before things would get sour between me and Nas. He was like Dr. Jekyll and Mr. Hyde. In addition to that, the SC controversy was still bubbling. Nas and SC had songs lyrically bashing and degrading each other, so I knew it wasn't over. Nas was about to drop a bomb. He told me he was working on a song and how he really took his time with this one. He just wanted to get everything off his chest. He had enough ammunition and was ready to fire away, but he was still worried. He was concerned for me and my reputation. We both knew that SC would attack me if he was challenged. It was never a question of what he'd say, but when he'd say it. I told Nas to do what he had to do and not to worry about me. What happened in the past happened, and I wasn't really concerned with what people thought of me. "Do what you have to do and say what you have to say," I repeated. I convinced Nas that I could handle anything SC threw my way. Although I considered SC to be my friend and had known him so well, I also knew that his ego would destroy our friendship.

In the meantime, Destiny was adjusting wonderfully. This was a perfect world in her eyes. She was so happy and content. I was very pleased with her new school. It was more down to earth than her previous school. Destiny instantly connected with her teacher as well. This was a huge relief for me. Destiny made a lot of new friends and turned out to be quite the social butterfly. She was estactic about living in such a huge home. She would rollerskate up and down the hallways and run and play. She was Alice in Wonderland. Surprisingly, Nas was home every night and was a little more attentive to our needs. He was trying and I could see as well as feel his efforts. "We" were trying. Without saying so, things seemed to just mesh together.

Once again, the Christmas holidays were right around the corner and I wanted to celebrate big! Destiny prepared her list and every day it was a countdown. My stepmother Melanie called me. She was amped! "Turn the radio on," she demanded.

I turned on the radio and heard Nas's new song "Ether." *Wow! Nas tore SC's ass up!* I thought. Later that night I went to visit Shelly. She had heard the song as well. I think *everyone* for that matter heard the song. It was the talk of the industry. She and I sat down and talked seriously about everything that was going on. I knew it was coming. I knew SC's cheap shot was coming. I was ready for whatever. I had no choice. Nas in the meantime was in his glory! His ego hadn't been stroked enough. His head was getting bigger by the minute. I was happy for him. He felt confident and it had been a long time since I saw a genuine smile on his face. He had battled and conquered. Nas proclaimed to have SC's life in the palm of his hands.

After "Ether," a new song emerged, "Supa Ugly." Just like we predicted, the entire song was a personal attack against me. I was at home, making preparations for the holiday, wrapping gifts, when suddenly Nas busted in. He was extremely excited, like he had just hit the lottery for billions.

"Carm, Carm, did you hear the song?"

"No, what song?"

"Your boyfriend's song. Yo, he's going at you the whole time. This nigga's a sucker!" he continued.

"What? What song?" I kept saying. I turned on the radio and tuned in to Hot 97.

I waited. Finally, Flex played "Ether," then played "Supa Ugly." I braced myself. I heard both versions and I yelled, "You gotta be fucking kidding me!" "Skeeted in Jeep/Left condoms in tha baby seat." Did this nigga just say he left used condoms in my daughter's baby seat? Wrong move! That was the moment I lost all respect for SC. Nas had won the battle.

I was so disgusted with SC. I was really hoping that he was the person he proclaimed to be. I guess he wasn't built for the business after all. His response was clearly an emotional one. It was an unwarranted attack. I had expected so much more from him. At first I was livid. Then once it finally settled in, I was hurt. For so long I had looked at SC like friend. I couldn't believe that he would sacrifice years of friendship for a battle that he ended up losing anyway.

My phone was ringing uncontrollably. My experiences in life were a clear picture to me that it was time that I commit to writing an autobiography. I had always wanted to write a book, and now was the perfect time. God was creating new experiences for me to fill my pages. It was amazing. Everything in my surroundings was happening for a reason. In fact, it got to the point where I no longer felt offended. Everything that was happening would be great for the book. Thanks to both SC and Nas the media pursuit was fascinating. The battle went on for a while which definitely helped Nas's career and record sales. SC ended up leaving the country on a retreat. Nas left town and went on a promotional tour to promote his new album, *Stillmatic*. It was the perfect time for me to start looking for a place.

CHAPTER 19

Point of No Return

• • • • • • • • •

IT WAS TIME TO start looking for my own place. I'd had a taste of freedom in Los Angeles and wouldn't be content until I was in my own space. After searching for weeks, I found a three-bedroom town house in a family-oriented Long Island community with a great school district and plenty of parks and beaches. I loved it but wasn't sure Destiny would. Nice as it was, the town house was no mansion, certainly no place for indoor roller-skating. From here on out, Destiny and I would comprise our family unit, so I needed her okay. We went to see it after school.

"Mommy, this is beautiful! Can we move in now? Are we going to take it?"

She ran upstairs and picked out her bedroom and designated the basement her playroom. With Destiny's approval, I signed the lease. We moved in February 2002.

Nas sold the mansion and relocated to New York City, taking Mrs. Jones with him. I suggested Nas move Mrs. Jones into his Atlanta home, but he claimed the house needed a few repairs before it would be livable and instead rented a two-bedroom apartment on the Upper East Side large enough for both of them. While Nas was on the road, Destiny and I kept Mrs. Jones company. Mrs. Jones found such pleasure in Destiny, her "little sunshine," and said that Destiny was the cute, articulate little girl she'd always wanted.

"Besides you, Mommy, Grandma Ann is the only other person that I can talk to," Destiny would often say. That probably had something to do with the fact that Mrs. Jones spoiled Destiny to no end. I'll never forget the time when Mrs. Jones fell asleep on the couch while watching TV and Destiny, who was about three at the time, slipped silently off the couch, found a pair of scissors and clipped away at her slumbering grandma's hair. When I came in the room, I couldn't believe my eyes.

"Destiny!" I shouted.

My high-pitched shriek startled Mrs. Jones out of sleep. When she realized what had happened, she brushed it off. "Don't yell at the baby, Carmen. It's okay," she said politely. I just laughed. In Mrs. Jones's eyes, Destiny could do no wrong. Indulgence is a grandmother's right, of course, but Mrs. Jones seemed to have mothered Nas with the same leniency. He grew up expecting an unconditional pardon from everyone, including me.

As winter gave way to spring, Mrs. Jones's health worsened, yet she and I bonded like never before. She confided her aspiration to start a jewelry business and a merchandising company for Nas. Above all, she wanted to live in a house and dreamed about a move down south where she also had relatives.

One visit, Mrs. Jones was especially talkative. "You know, Carmen, we've known each other for a long time and I want you to know that no matter what we've been through, I love you and Destiny very much and I will always watch after ya'll, no matter where I am."

I was speechless. My strained relationship with Mrs. Jones went way back to my stay with her in Queensbridge. I always felt that she never "got" me and knew that she saw me as a threat to her bond with Nas. I asked myself why I hadn't tried harder. Why had I let often trivial issues prevent our closeness?

"Oh, Mrs. Jones, you ain't goin' nowhere. You're going to be fine. Destiny and I will be back in a couple of days." I gave her a hug and kiss, and we left.

That evening I called Nas. "Look, I don't care where you're at or what you're doing, get your ass home fast! Your mother isn't looking or sounding too good."

A couple of days later Destiny and I headed into the city to visit with Mrs. Jones. On the way we bought fresh vegetables, fruit and bottled water. Mrs. Jones loved her live enzymes and fresh food, always careful of what she put in her body. When we arrived, the doorman informed us that Mrs. Jones had been taken to a nearby hospital by ambulance. We were all aware of her condition but I wasn't prepared for this. I had to be strong for Destiny. Destiny gripped my hand and I squeezed hers even tighter for support.

I called Nas and left him several messages before he returned my call. When I finally spoke to him, he let me know which hospital Mrs. Jones was in and that he was on his way.

The following day Destiny and I met Nas at the hospital. We entered and were welcomed by security and then directed to elevators. The moment I stepped off of the elevator my walk became heavy as though a million bricks were strapped to my feet. I was so scared. Scared of seeing Mrs. Jones in poor condition and even more afraid of what Destiny's reaction would be. Mrs. Jones was in a semi-private room so I suggested to Nas that he get her a private room. I knew she would be much more comfortable. Nas took care of it and by the next day Mrs. Jones was in her own room with a beautiful view of the 59th Street Bridge. Ironically, from her bed she could view Queensbridge. With the help of some well-deserved rest, by the next day her complexion looked a lot healthier than it had the day before. She was talking and moving around better than she had been. She seemed to be feeling a whole lot better. But Nas was a nervous wreck.

His mother's condition was Nas's number one concern, but there was so much going on around him. His career had resurrected. He was working hard and I could tell that all of the SC controversy was still bothering him. It was a lot for one person to deal with and like most men, Nas channeled his thoughts and emotions into work. Destiny and I were visiting Mrs. Jones at the hospital every day. Nas came through when he could, which wasn't too often, because he was touring. That also was the case with Jabari. Unfortunately they were the only ones who could make decisions on their mother's behalf, so their absence made things difficult.

When Nas finally showed up, Papa Lenny, who had been visiting with Mrs. Jones, let him have it.

"Look, one of you niggas gotta be here, Nas, this don't make no sense. Your mother is sick and the doctors need to speak to you or Jabari. Come on, man!"

Nas stayed by his mother's side the duration of the day. Later on that evening Nas's uncle and cousin came by the hospital. They had taken the train up from South Carolina. Mrs. Jones was asleep when they arrived.

We were all talking softly in her room, when Nas's cousin came out of nowhere and said, "Nas, you got a place for us to sleep? Can you put us up in a hotel?" Nas didn't answer. His uncle chimed in, "And we ain't got no clothes either. We need some new clothes and sneakers." If looks could kill they both would have been dead. Nas jumped up and left the room. Minutes later Jabari entered and motioned for them both to follow him. They did. Jabari drove them right back to the train station, dropped them off and returned to the hospital.

Nas stayed overnight at the hospital. The following day the doctor announced that it would be best to release Mrs. Jones to a hospice. There was nothing more they could do for her and it was only a matter of time now. No one was prepared for this, especially Destiny. Her Grandma Ann was her best friend in the whole wide world. I was extremely concerned about how all this would affect her. Later that evening I went to see Nas to tell him what the doctor had suggested. He refused to talk about it. I think he was in denial. When I explained the purpose of a hospice, he still seemed detached. I guess his way of dealing with the situation was to simply ignore it. Nas viciously screamed, "Look, I have a lot on my mind right now. They want me to do the J.Lo video in a few days. I'm leaving to go back out on the road soon. I can't take all of this." I took a minute to digest his words then said, "Fuck a J.Lo video. Do you think if J.Lo's mother was in this condition she'd be giving two shits about a Nas video? Her whole world would be shut down, trust me." That was it for me. I was fuming. I couldn't believe what I was hearing. I knew at that moment that I had made a wise choice when I broke up with Nas. How a man treats his mother is how he will eventually treat his wife. I'm not saying Nas wasn't a good son, but I will say she deserved more than she received. I was dealing with my own issues. I was feeling extremely guilty about some of the things I used to say and do in the past. I was sorry for them now and the more frustrated I got the more I blamed Nas. I couldn't turn back the hands of time and I was angry.

At home I picked up *Conversations with God.* Reading it for a second time was perhaps less revelatory but more comforting, especially with the gravity of Mrs. Jones's condition. I stayed up until dawn and finally fell asleep just before the alarm clock sounded. When I woke up, I thought of Mrs. Jones. Later that day, Nas paged me. Mrs. Jones had passed away.

Destiny took it hard, very hard. It would be a long time before she'd be able to say her grandma's name without crying. After the wake, I called to check on Nas, thinking he and Destiny might benefit from spending some time together. But Nas was too busy, he said. He was up in Spanish Harlem filming the video for J.Lo's single, "I'm Gonna Be Alright." Destiny and I were not invited to the funeral service, which was held the following day in North Carolina. So my sister Nini and I worked to distract Destiny, and little by little, we convinced her that she would be okay.

. . .

The months were rolling by. Nas was working on a new album and really feeling himself. During a live radio interview Nas made a comment about Cam'ron's current album at the time, *Come Home with Me*. He said it was trash and that Cam'ron should change his name from "Cam'ron to Can't Rhyme." Cam retaliated with "Killa's Revenge." *Here we go again,* I thought. Although Nas was completely out of line for making that comment about Cam'ron's album, I couldn't understand why Cam came after me and Destiny.

"Tell ya daughter R. Kelly/Have my way with her face" were the lyrics that enraged me and had me on a verbal rampage. Cam also displayed poor taste when he talked disrespectfully about Mrs. Jones, whom we had just lost. I was even more surprised that Hot 97 supported the song. Say what you feel about me, but leave my child out of it! Then I received a call from a good friend, Charles Fisher, who worked with the Hip Hop Summit. He asked if Nas, Destiny and I would be interested in attending a sit-down with Cam'ron and a few executives from Def Jam including Russell Simmons. He also mentioned that the media would be invited to attend to witness the truce. He even suggested that Cam'ron pick Destiny up in front of the cameras as he apologized. *"What?* If that nigga Cam'ron comes anywhere near my daughter, I'm putting a bullet in his fucking forehead. I'm not Nas, I'll do the twenty-five to life!"

Charles was cool and I had absolutely no problems with him, but I was still infuriated by Cam'ron's statements. It was just bad timing on Charles's part. At that point I decided to hold a press conference and put an end to it all. De Spa, located on 139th Street and 8th Avenue in Striver's Row, supported and welcomed my press conference. The charade had gone on long enough. Everyone invited appeared. Writers from several different magazines as well as broadcasters from Channel 9 and BET were present. I read my statement in defense of my daughter and left. Of course, Nas didn't want me to do the press conference. He insisted he would take care of it, but I knew there was nothing he could do.

• • •

During this time, my relationship with Nas was pretty much the same—back and forth. We were still intimate and entertained each other on occasion. Nas still wanted to get married and move to the mystery house in Atlanta. Every so often he would propose and I would decline. He was still touring and from time to time he would send for Destiny and me, which was new. We always had fun and I could see a slight change in Nas, but still I did not want to be in a relationship with him. I was cool with hanging out once in a while, but that was it. Nas, on the other hand, was adamant about getting married. He wanted us to have more children and move far away. I desired the same things, just not with him.

"Carm, when are you going to let me back in? I want to come home to you and Des and eat broiled salmon and rice too. I want to wake up to you getting Destiny ready for school. Carm, I want my family back," he pleaded. But as much as I wanted to, I just couldn't give Nas what he desired.

Family life with Nas would be exactly what it had always been: Me being miserable, stuck in the house doing everything while he came and went as he pleased. He was way too comfortable with me. So I did what I needed to do. Although Nas was hurt he also understood. He knew deep down we had no future, but never stopped beating a dead horse. The chances of us getting married and having a larger family were slim to none but he just wouldn't give up.

One Sunday after visiting with her dad, Destiny went on and on about what a great time she had over the weekend. In the midst of our conversation, she mentioned her dad's new friend. "Mommy, I met Daddy's new friend, she's cool. I like her. I forgot her name, but she has a really curly, like afro hairstyle and she had gold teeth.

"What's her name?"

"I think her name is Kerri, I don't remember." Nas had never mentioned Kerri, whose name actually turned out to be Kelis. Not that he was obligated to tell me, but if he has our child around another woman who is significant in his life I need to know. When I asked about it, his response was, "That's not my girl, so why mention her?" I had heard something about them seeing each other on the radio but I think it was an uncomfortable situation for Nas. This clearly told me that he was still up to his old tricks. So I said, "Nas obviously you like this girl if you introduced her to our daughter. What's the problem, why can't you just keep it real?

"Naw, she mess with Puff too, I ain't wife-n her. I told you she ain't my girl." I left it at that.

After that things between Nas and me stayed the same. "Nas, when I'm ready to marry you, I'll propose to you. Please stop asking."

Thanksgiving was right around the corner. Nas wanted Destiny and me to spend the holiday with him in Atlanta at the new house. "Come on, Carm, I want you to cook your famous macaroni and cheese and candied yams, let's be a family this Thanksgiving." I had to decline. I knew that once we got to Atlanta, Destiny would love the new house, and I would be put in a position that I really didn't care to be in. Nas was upset, but he took it in stride.

Another Christmas rolled in and the house was decorated, the tree had all the trimmings and bright lights. I cooked a big dinner and Destiny was excited to open her gifts. This year Destiny wanted nothing but Bratz dolls and all the accessories. She loved to do makeovers and was a pro at painting their faces. After opening all of her gifts Des and I snacked, played, watched videos and even took a nap.

Shortly after, she asked about her father. I suggested she give him a call. Nas wasn't feeling too good and said he would stop by later. A couple of hours passed. No Nas. Destiny stood firm on his word. She sat at the window and watched as cars bypassed our house, hoping that one of the passing cars could perhaps be her dad, but he never came. I paced briskly. I was furious. It was 8 P.M. when he finally called. I let him have it and then I hung up on him. Exactly forty-five minutes later he was ringing the bell bearing gifts for Destiny. For me he had much attitude, which I expected and could care less about. A few hours passed and Destiny was finally winding down. I bathed her and put her to bed. The house was a mess; toys were everywhere, gifts were sorted across the living room floor, remnants of Christmas dinner still lingered on the table. I had my work cut out for me. I started cleaning immediately. Nas hung around and surprisingly his nasty attitude toward me had disappeared. I felt him close behind me. I ignored him. Then he grabbed me. His protruding manhood grinded against me.

"Stop it, Nas!" I shouted. "Stop! Nas, what are you doing? Get off of me." He kept pulling me close to him, but I eventually broke loose and ran upstairs. He was right on my trail.

My bedroom was dark, but I knew my way around. He threw me on the bed and raised my dress. I was turned off, he was overly aggressive. I resisted as long as I could. Two minutes later, I felt violated and used. "Get out!" I screamed.

Nas just sucked his teeth. "I pay the rent up here, I'm not going nowhere. And if I catch a nigga up in here, I'm fucking him up." He left shortly after. I never felt such disgust and disgrace.

CHAPTER 20

Fatal Attraction

· · · · · · · · · ·

IT WAS THE DAY before New Year's Eve when I heard that Puffy was having a party in Miami. I called Shelly and although it was last minute, we manged to to get it together. Shelly called a connect of hers to get us event passes. After we landed and checked in our hotel, we hit the strip. This was going to be a fun night.

The whole scene reminded me of a masquerade ball, very exotic for the dead of winter. We maneuvered our way through the crowd and made it to the bar, ordered our drinks, which of course were on the house, and headed up to the VIP section. "Shelly, what the hell do you think you're doing?"

And she replied, "I just took a half an X. It's New Year's."

Seconds to midnight, Puff grabbed the microphone and screamed, "Five, four, three, two, one . . . Happy New Year." The entire club joined in celebration and for at least another hour everyone was drowning themselves in alcohol.

When I returned to New York, Nas was touring Europe and called every night. He was lonely and missed his family. Although Nas and I had lots of drama, we still loved each other. Again, I wasn't in love, but I had love for him. One evening we spoke on the phone and he asked me if I still wanted to have more children. Nas had good intentions, but his efforts never matched his words. He said that he was a changed man and was ready to settle down. I wished him the best and suggested he find what he was looking for with his new girlfriend, Kelis. I said, "If you can't be with the one you love, Nas, you might as well love the one you're with. Be faithful for once in your life." He responded with "You know me, Carm, I can't help it. I just love women." It seemed like he wanted me all to himself while he was free to share himself with others.

We talked for a long time this particular evening. Then he asked, "Carm, is there any possibility of us getting back together?"

"You want the truth, Nas? No. We can be friends. We can even be lovers. I can't trust you enough to be more than that. I mean, you didn't even tell me that you were engaged. I had to hear it on the radio. Don't do her like you did me, Nas." The conversation ended on a somber note.

Two weeks later Nas returned from Europe. Immediately after his flight landed, he was at my door. It was around eleven and Destiny was fast asleep. I fixed him a plate of leftovers, we talked for a while, then we both retired to the bedroom. The entire time, his cell phone was ringing off the hook. I thought quickly to myself, at one time that used to be me. The phone kept ringing, but he refused to answer it or turn it off so it rang all night, literally.

That next morning, Destiny woke up and was so excited to see her father. They ate breakfast together, then we dropped her off at school. I then gave Nas a ride to the city. On the way, his phone rang repeatedly. "Who is that calling you like that?" I asked.

"It's Kelis," he answered. "I know she's going to be mad. She knows I flew in last night."

I shook my head and said, "Answer it, Nas, or she'll keep calling." So he finally did. He gave her some lame excuse about being in a meeting. I thought to myself, *Yeah right, at eight o'clock in the morning. That's the dumb shit he used to tell me.*

When he hung up with her I just shook my head like, been there, done that! Then he called two of his friends and instructed them to pick up some weed and meet him at his apartment in Manhattan. Typical nigga! I dropped him off and went on about my business.

While I was evolving in my world, my little Destiny was doing some evolving on her own. She was growing into a young lady, claiming her own identity. She was known as the popular girl in school which boosted her self-esteem far beyond imagination, but in a good way. Destiny adored her friends and often had company. That was fine with me, as long as her homework was completed. I enjoyed baking cookies and making treats and joining in on the activities every once in a while.

Summer was right around the corner and the days were getting warmer and warmer. Shelly and I decided to meet for lunch and play catch up. We settled on one of my favorite Jamaican restaurants, The Door in Queens. We both ordered the brown stew chicken with rice and peas and shared a carafe of fruit punch. After placing our order, my cell rang. It was Nas.

"Hey, what's up, where you at?"

"Nothing much, I'm having lunch with Shelly," I said.

"Oh word, tell Shell I said what's up. I called because I want to know if you and Des want to spend the fourth of July with me in Miami. I'm renting a little yacht, nothing big. It's gonna be real nice. So ya'll wanna come?" he asked.

I wanted to jump at the invitation, but I knew Nas had a hidden agenda. Traveling is one of my weaknessess, so I thought for a quick moment then declined the offer.

"The ride is over, Nas. I'll bring Destiny, but I'm not hanging out with you." It was clear that Nas was in a new relationship playing old games, and I really didn't have time for the bullshit. Nas then went on about how he missed his family and wished things could go back to the way they used to be. "Carm, I just want to hold you. Please come to Miami. It will be fun." At that point I was ready to get off the phone. I had to hang up.

"Let me call you back. My food just arrived," I said hurriedly. When I got off the phone I told Shelly about our conversation and asked what she thought. "Where is Kelis?" she said.

"He never mentioned her at all, I don't know where she is," I replied. Just then I got a message from Nas on my two-way. It read "Don't forget to bring a thong and some toys." I showed the message to Shelly, who was about to explode with laughter. I texted him back; "I don't think so. Dust ya-self off and try again."

After light conversation and a good meal, I thought about Nas. Despite our ups and downs we had years of history together. I had to accept the fact that we would be connected for forever. So I gave in and decided that I would fly Destiny to Miami so that she could spend some quality time with her father. When we arrived at the airport I was surprised to see Nas and Kelis standing there. Nas didn't look pleased. He had an attitude, his face was tight with tension, and I could feel his energy before he spoke. He attempted to introduce us, but by that time Kelis and I had already greeted each other with a hug and a smile. I immediately was thrown off by an unpleasant smell. *Wow,* I thought, *somebody forgot to put on deodorant.*

I had already heard so much about Kelis from Destiny. She was very cordial and pleasant. When we got in the car I noticed that we were heading downtown. "Where are we going?" I asked. "Nas, I thought we agreed that I would stay on the beach for the weekend."

Kelis took the liberty to speak on his behalf. "Well, since it was short notice and we didn't know you were coming until yesterday, we couldn't get you a room on the beach. Everything was booked."

"Yesterday?" I said. Then I thought, *Carm, don't blow up the spot.* "So then where am I staying?" I asked.

Nas replied, "You're staying at the same hotel as us. Downtown!"

What the fuck is going on? I thought to myself. Maintaining my composure, I two-wayed Nas who was sitting directly in front of me. The text read: "WHAT IS GOING ON? I AM NOT STAYING DOWNTOWN IN YOUR HOTEL FOR THE WEEKEND. I DON'T KNOW WHAT Y'ALL ARE TRYING TO PULL BUT TELL THE DRIVER TO HIT COLLINS AND WE WILL FIND A HOTEL, AND I'M NOT EVEN KIDDING."

Shortly after, we were in the lobby of the Palm Hotel on Collins. While Kelis was getting my room, Nas and I argued. The whole purpose of us flying down was for me to drop Destiny off with her father so that they could spend some time together. I guess I had spoiled Nas's original plans and now he was trying to leave Destiny with me.

"What's really good, Nas? Why don't you want to take Destiny with you? Why are we here? I brought her to Miami to be with you," I argued. He said that he had plans for the evening and all this other bullshit. Kelis came over and added her two cents. I was so upset with Nas that I didn't bother to entertain Kelis. "Nas, you better tell her, I'm not the one."

"Well, Carm, you haven't been letting Nas see his daughter since he and I got together," Kelis responded. I had to laugh.

"What? Is that what you told her, Uncle Daddy? That I keep you from your daughter?" It was obvious he was filling her head with lots of bull and that she was rather naïve when it came to Nas.

When I threatened to pull out my two-way, Nas immediately changed his tone and Kelis conveniently walked away. The truth hurts and I was about to blow shit up! I had evidence that Nas was full of shit and the proof was right in my hands, just a push of a button away. Nas changed his mind a few seconds later and decided to take Destiny as planned. I felt horrible that she had to witness such behavior. She was almost in tears as she sat on the couch in the lobby. All she knew was that she had flown to Florida to be with her father and that somehow the plans had changed without explanation. The drama ended with Nas leaving with Destiny and Kelis. I proceeded to my room.

I took a warm bath and meditated. I needed to calm my spirits and focus on positive energy. I ordered a bottle of wine, drank it and passed out. The following day, I cut my trip short and flew back to New York. I felt completely naked without Destiny. She was my little partner and even though it had only been a couple of days, I missed her dearly. A few days later Destiny finally called. I was so surprised to hear her crying on the other end of the phone. Apparently Kelis was playing the stepmother role and was feelin' herself. The new house rule was no thumbsucking, and it affected Destiny a great deal.

• • •

The summer was winding down, and fall was a few days away. Shelly and I decided to go to the city for a nice dinner and a few drinks. When I got to Shelly's she wasn't ready, which was usual so I went upstairs for a few minutes. When we came downstairs my car was gone. My baby was gone! There was shattered glass and metal on the ground adjacent to where I had parked. Shelly immediately called the police and they arrived in minutes. They asked a lot of questions about Nas, who was the insurance holder. I told them everything I knew. One officer began to inquire about my personal relationship with Nas. I explained to him that we were no longer together, but that we were cool. He just started laughing. "I'm sorry, no disrespect, but I see this all the time."

"See what?" I replied.

"Couples break up and have each other's possessions stolen or destroyed out of pure spite," he said.

"Nah, Nas wouldn't do that, he's not that kind of person," I said. I was so upset that I couldn't think straight. What was I going to do without a car? Who the fuck stole my car? I thought about what the cop said but I knew there was no way that Nas could be responsible for having my car stolen.

The following day, I called Nas's business manager and gave him all the information needed to file for the insurance claim. He assured me that when the check arrived he would forward it to Nas so that I could purchase another vehicle. Meanwhile I rented a car from a local dealer. The rental was way out of my budget and I didn't know how I was going to pay for it. After two months, I fell behind with my payments and the dealer wanted the car returned. I called Nas and inquired about the insurance check, it had to be in by now. I found out from Nas that the check had arrived weeks ago. He said he had no intentions on giving me a dime toward transportation. He said, "This is my money, Carm, and you are on your own. Get one of them niggas you fuck with to buy you a ride."

"What-eva, nigga, we'll be all right. Keep the insurance check, it's obvious you need it," I said and hung up the phone. My rental was due back in two days, I was broke and depressed, but more important I was sick to my stomach with disgust for Nas. It was what it was and I had no choice but to accept it. I knew that Nas was still bitter about the whole SC episode and couldn't deal with the fact that even after all of that, I still didn't want to be with him. Nas's ego had waged a war against me and there was no surrender. I was back to square one—broke, carless, jobless, but far from hopeless!

CHAPTER 21

Uncle Daddy

. . . .

I FOUND THE STRENGTH to proceed quietly and cautiously with help and guidance from God. My routine resumed and when possible I stayed clear of Nas. I didn't need any more unnecessary drama. I needed to get refocused. Shelly called one evening and informed me that Tone from Track Masters was having a birthday party. The party was at an intimate Middle Eastern lounge. It was a beautiful setting, very cozy and intimate, with lots of couches and big fluffy decorated pillows. Silk scarves draped from the ceiling, which gave an ultra sexy feel to the place. The waitresses wore sexy little genie outfits and Tunisian music played softly in the background. It was very exotic. I was feeling the energy all around.

Shelly and I wanted to remain low profile so we sat in a secluded area and observed the scene from a distance. Steve

Stoute came over with a bottle of champagne and a few glasses. We talked for a while, though I was careful to avoid any delicate topics, since it seemed with Steve sensitive information got back to Nas. Steve was suddenly distracted by a new arrival at the club and rushed off without even excusing himself. I looked over to find he'd dashed off to greet none other than SC. It was like seeing a ghost. I knew we would eventually bump heads but never imagined it would happen that night.

Shelly noticed my hypnotic gaze in SC's direction. "You better not say shit to that nigga," Shelly whispered. "Fuck that nigga."

"Shell, please, you ain't got to tell me." However, avoiding eye contact was a struggle since he stared at me continuously. I finally gave up and looked him dead in the eyes. What, SC? He cracked a smile, an incomprehensible grin that could have been so many different things: a smile of regret, a smile of friendship. Shelly elbowed me hard in the side and sucked her teeth. It was definitely time to hit the ladies room.

"Carm, what the fuck was he smiling at?" she yelled.

"I know, right?" It felt so unnatural to see SC and not speak. I had to gather myself. When we came out of the bathroom, SC and Steve were gone. What a relief. After I dropped Shelly in Queens, I took the long haul back to Long Island. Home was on the horizon when Musiq's "Half Crazy" came on the radio. I'd heard the song plenty of times. Tonight I opened my ears and really listened.

> *Now things are strange, nothing's the same*
> *And really I just want my friend back*

I revisited my past with SC. I thought of all the moments we'd shared, both good and bad. The pain I'd tucked away was ready to be released. I finally cried, sitting in my driveway for half an hour before I went inside. It felt great to finally let it all out. The next morning, I woke up feeling like a new person.

. . .

It was a Friday evening when Nas called. He was in Florida, exactly fifteen minutes from South Beach, working on his double album. In the midst of me going off on him about not showing up to court for a custody and visitation hearing, he asked if I could bring Destiny down to see him. Months prior, Nas had taken Destiny out of state without my knowledge or permission. I was worried sick when she never made it home Sunday and I couldn't get in touch with Nas. When he brought her home that Monday afternoon, I was an emotional wreck. Nas dismissed my anger as if I had no reason to be so upset. To prevent the situation from ever recurring, I filed for a custody/visitation order, which would ultimately be granted.

Nas continued saying he missed Destiny and wanted to spend quality time with her. *Here we go again,* I thought. I knew there would be a chance I'd have to take this one, even if it was bullshit. I was mentally tired and I knew Destiny wanted to see her father. She had recess coming up, so I agreed. Nas then asked if I could hang out as well. He said that he was in the middle of his project and could use the help with Destiny. I agreed with his request and a few days later Destiny and I boarded the flight to Miami.

The flight was smooth. Aw! Florida! A breath of fresh air. It felt so tropical. The hotel was beautiful and was directly across the street from Bal Harbour Mall. Nas also sprung a big surprise on me. We were all staying in the same suite, because the hotel was booked solid. I was not happy with the arrangement, but again, I didn't want to argue so I compromised and went along with it. Destiny was so overjoyed and I didn't want to spoil her high.

Nas and I spent our days at the pool sipping on cocktails while Destiny played close by. He mentioned that his girlfriend Kelis was giving him a hard time about me being in Florida with him. As I listened it became obvious this was something routine with Kelis. A few cocktails later, Nas was lit up. Actually we both were. We went upstairs for a quickie and it was the one of the best quickies we had ever had. We came back downstairs by the poolside and continued to talk. Being friends/lovers wouldn't be so bad. No strings attached, so I thought.

Summer was right around the corner. Nas felt guilty about my transportation situation and ended up buying us a little black Jeep. I was happy to be able to get around. I pushed for a BMW, but my friends at the dealership made it very clear that although Nas didn't have a problem with it, Kelis did. She didn't even want Nas to buy us the Jeep. I understood and left matters alone. Destiny and I took our first long-distance drive to Atlanta in our new car. We were visiting Shelly, who had recently relo- cated to the south. Nas was also now living in Atlanta so it was perfect. Destiny could spend time with her dad. I talked to Nas on my cell phone most of the ride. As the conversation took off,

I adjusted the radio and found one of my favorite songs, "The Best of Me," by Mya. Humming along while listening to Nas, I stumbled over the lyrics.

"What did you just say?"

"I said, would you have a threesome with me and Kelis?" he repeated.

"What? Hell no!" I was so completely thrown off by his request that I even had to laugh. I thought, *He's got to be joking.* But he wasn't, he was dead serious.

"Why not?" he kept asking as if my answer would change.

"No! Nas, you have never in your life asked me no shit like that before. What's the problem?" I asked.

"There is no problem, that's just something I want to do. That's my fantasy," he explained. "How about you come with me to the strip club when you get here?"

I ended the conversation and hung up. As I drove I thought about our conversation. I was still in shock. Where was all this coming from? After a twelve-hour ride we finally pulled into Georgia.

• • •

Weeks had gone by when I took a trip to New York for our court appearance. There was still the unsettled matter regarding visitation. Once again, Nas was a no-show. I went home to check on things and then drove back to Atlanta. I had such a good time in the city and really wasn't ready to leave, but when summer ended it was time to get Destiny back to school in New York. As I was packing, Nas called and asked if he could take me out.

"I'm not going to no strip club, Nas!" I said.

"I don't want to take you to a strip club, Carm, I just want to get something to eat."

What did I have to lose? He picked me up from Shelly's and we drove around for a while looking for a restaurant. It was late and most of the restaurants were closed so we drove back to Shelly's crib and picked up a bottle of wine on the way. Then we made another detour, and this time we ended up at the Hilton Hotel in Alpharetta. Nas's driver/bodyguard went inside and returned five minutes later with a key. We went up to the room, got pissy drunk and before I knew it we were getting it popping. Having sex with Nas was second nature; I didn't feel like I was giving in. Old habits really are hard to break.

The next morning, he asked me again, "Carm, please will you have a threesome with us?"

"Why, Nas? Why do you want to have a threesome with me? Out of all the women in this world you mean to tell me that the two of you can't find anyone else?"

"Because, Carm, I want both my bitches at the same time."

I stopped dead in my tracks. "I'm not your bitch!"

"Yes, you are and you will always be," Nas insisted. That was all I needed to hear. That would be our last episode. We'd never have sex again.

"What does your girlfriend think about this?" I had to ask.

"She'll do whatever I ask her to do. She said she's never had a threesome before but if I wanted to she would," he claimed.

"But does she know that you're asking me to do it with you?"

"No. I mean, we talked about it, but I didn't tell her I wanted it to be with you. That's why I want ya'll to be cool, this way we can all hang out. Why don't you come out to lunch with us one day, so we can all just, you know, be cool?"

"No! I'm not interested, Nas, so please just stop asking me!"

Court dates came and went and still no Nas. One weekend Nas came to get Destiny, and even though I felt it was a little risky, I agreed to the visit. His visits with her were few and far between and I knew she missed him. This time he brought Kelis with him, who looked aggravated, her face set hard and tight. We greeted one another and Destiny left with them. Sunday rolled around and Nas brought Destiny home. She said that as soon as they had all gotten in the car two days earlier, Kelis had begun to talk about me.

"What did she say?" I asked.

"Mommy, she said that you're not doing anything, and that you were busy doing nothing," Destiny whined.

I soothed her. "Des, Kelis is just being Kelis. Don't worry about her. Don't let the little things bother you."

Destiny and I had no beef with Kelis for the first year she was seeing Nas. I actually felt she provided a stabilizing influence on Nas, making Destiny's visits with him more secure and fun. But then I got a phone call from Destiny on one of her visits, asking to come home. She said her daddy was letting Kelis be mean to her and boss her around. Kelis had gotten a little beside herself with the future stepmother role, attempting to break Destiny of her thumb-sucking habit and going about it the wrong way.

There are always issues when a childless person enters into a relationship with a person who already has a child. Until you have kids of your own, you might not possess the sensitivity necessary to deal with them correctly. I tried to address the situation with Nas, but he played dumb. He enjoyed the spectacle of his daughter and girlfriend fighting, since he somehow believed they were fighting over him. It was just the first of many instances in which Destiny would be intimidated by Kelis, who now had the leading position in Nas's life.

As Christmas 2004 approached, I called Nas to asked for the usual amount of shopping money. Kelis answered and at that point I couldn't hold it in. "You're not fooling anyone, you better relax around my daughter. And by the way, I'm not interested in having a threesome with you and Nas, so back off, bitch!"

She didn't seem surprised with my tone. "Oh really, he asked you to have a threesome? Well, do you enjoy having sex with my man? I love it."

"Okay, so he satisfies you, but the real question is, do you satisfy him? That's what you should be asking yourself. Obviously not, if he's begging me to show you how it's done!"

She hung up the phone. The following day Destiny tried calling her dad and the number had been changed. Days went by and he eventually called and gave us the new number. He had a callous attitude and said that he wasn't giving me a dime to shop for Destiny this Christmas. A week later, Nas's accountant called and said that Nas would no longer be paying child support. Another phone call came from Rick at Power Motors, asking me to return the Jeep since Nas's checks had been bouncing. He'd actually been letting me drive the Jeep for six months without paying a red cent. Things went from terrible to horrible.

I called Nas immediately. "Nas, I just got a call from my land-lord. He said you stopped paying the rent. Do you want to explain that?"

"Carm, call me during business hours, Monday through Friday," he said in a barely civil tone.

"First of all, you are far from a businessman. You rhyme for a living. Therefore it shouldn't make a difference when I call you, weekend or weekday. You don't have nothing going on. No office, no staff, no nothing. This is about our daughter. Do you really think that you can just stop paying child support?"

He heaved a world-weary sigh and said, "You only call me for money and you look at me like a fucking check."

"So what? Why do you care how I look at you? It's not about us. It's about Destiny. You stopped sending the support checks, stopped paying for the car, and now you stopped paying the rent."

There was no reasoning with him. The following Monday I went back to family court and filed for child support.

• • •

The first Thursday after the New Year, Nas called. He and Kelis were getting married and Saturday was the big day.

"You're getting married in two days and you're just calling?" I asked.

"I want Destiny to fly to Atlanta for the wedding," he said harshly. "I'm making arrangements." Nas was famous for doing things at the last minute. It was short notice, but could be worked out. "I want her to fly down with my pops."

"That's not a good idea, Nas. Destiny has only been in Olu's presence a mere three times in her whole life. He's a stranger to her. I can't even remember the last time he called to speak to her. He's not in her life like that. Get us the tickets and I will escort her down."

"I can't afford the extra ticket, but I'll try."

"You should be able to afford it. It's not like you're paying child support."

He put me on hold for a few minutes. He came back on the line with a brusque statement. "The tickets will be delivered in the morning."

By Friday evening there were still no tickets. I told Destiny we could drive down to the wedding in my sister Nini's car if she really wanted to go. But when she found out that her cousins, Jabari's kids, weren't invited to the wedding at all, she decided to stay home, too. At first she wasn't mad at Nas.

"Mommy, don't be mad at Daddy," she said. "He's not rich anymore."

It broke my heart to see her making excuses for her father and surrendering so easily to missing his wedding. Expectations are necessary for disappointment and Destiny had no expectations from her father. Of course Nas's career had gotten Destiny used to his absences.

Destiny was also beginning to recognize his double standards. She saw the video for "I Can," which featured Nas surrounded by kids, encouraging them to pursue their dreams. In fact, years before he had flown into a rage when he learned that Destiny had appeared in a video for the R&B group Total. Tracey invited me to the video shoot, which Puff was producing. He asked Destiny to do a scene with his son Justin for the video's end. In the scene they hugged and kissed, two four-year-olds in a gesture of innocence and sweetness. Destiny had been so excited to tell Nas that she'd been in a video just like him. His response was anger that I'd allowed her participation. Kids have a surprising way of remembering things, and Destiny still recalled his anger about the Total video when she saw "I Can" years later.

So Destiny was accustomed to her father's hypocrisy and took missing his wedding in stride—until we learned the identity of the flower girl. Nas's father's niece's daughter had the honor of preceding Kelis up the aisle. Nas's second cousin had been featured in the ceremony while his own daughter's invitation to the event was a mere afterthought. "I should have been the first one on the list," she said, finally. I was relieved. I didn't want Destiny to be angry with her father, but anger was better than calm acceptance of mistreatment.

The next time Nas showed up to see Destiny, I let him in and offered him a seat in the living room where he chatted with Destiny for a while. When it was time for him to leave, my sister Nini served him a summons to appear in court. If he wasn't going to respect my gangsta, he needed to respect the courts. It was the only way he'd ever take care of his responsibilities.

Nas showed up in court this time, flanked by Kelis and his attorney. Papa Lenny and Nini came with me for support, though I was officially representing myself.

We were escorted to a conference room and got down to

business. Nas was ordered to pay exactly what he had been paying for a temporary period.

As we left the conference room, we were ambushed by
Celebrity Court TV. Nas rushed past them, refusing to turn
around and give an interview.

"Hey, Nas," the press yelled. "Nas!"

"Dammit, I need a frontal on Nas," a cameraman complained.

Papa Lenny knew just what to do. "Hey, Nas," he called. At
the sound of a familiar voice, Nas turned around.

"Thanks," the cameraman said, after Nas and Kelis finally escaped. "That's just what we needed."

Papa Lenny was good for one more thing that day: He made
the acquaintance of an attorney named Wayne Marks, whom I
immediately hired. Though my child support had been rein-
stated, my eviction notice still remained to be dealt with. My new
lawyer made arrangements with Nas's attorney to get the back
rent paid and the next day I received a certified check via FedEx.
I took care of my business and settled things with my landlord.

In October 2005, SC and Nas united onstage in a symbolic
end to their beef. Soon the news broke that Nas was signing a
record deal with Def Jam.

In the meantime, we were set to go back to court over permanent child support. My lawyer and I subpoenaed Rick of Power
Motors, Steve Stoute, Jacob the Jeweler and numerous other
associates of Nas. He quickly settled, uncomfortable with the
prospect of airing all his financial information. The permanent
court-ordered support went into effect on December 1, 2005. I

felt that Nas put Destiny through a lot of strife just to fight me in a battle that he knew I'd win anyway. The support was important for Destiny's well-being. She deserved to live the life she was accustomed to, despite the dissolvement of our relationship.

At the end of the day I have come to know what I consider the three most valuable lessons in life. One, nothing is a coincidence. The people you meet in the walk of everyday life, you meet for a reason. Two, there are no victims and no villains in this world. And last but not least, *love* conquers all!

And I am still growing so . . . the saga continues.